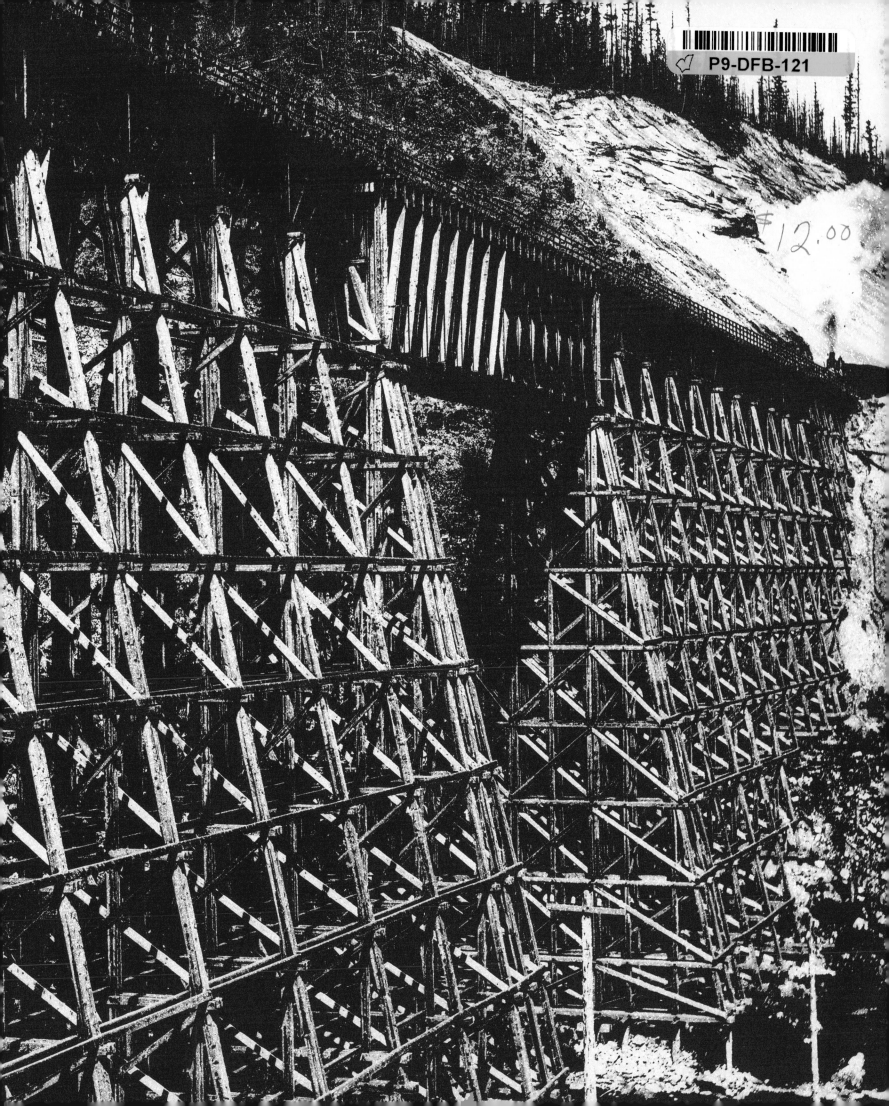

$12.00

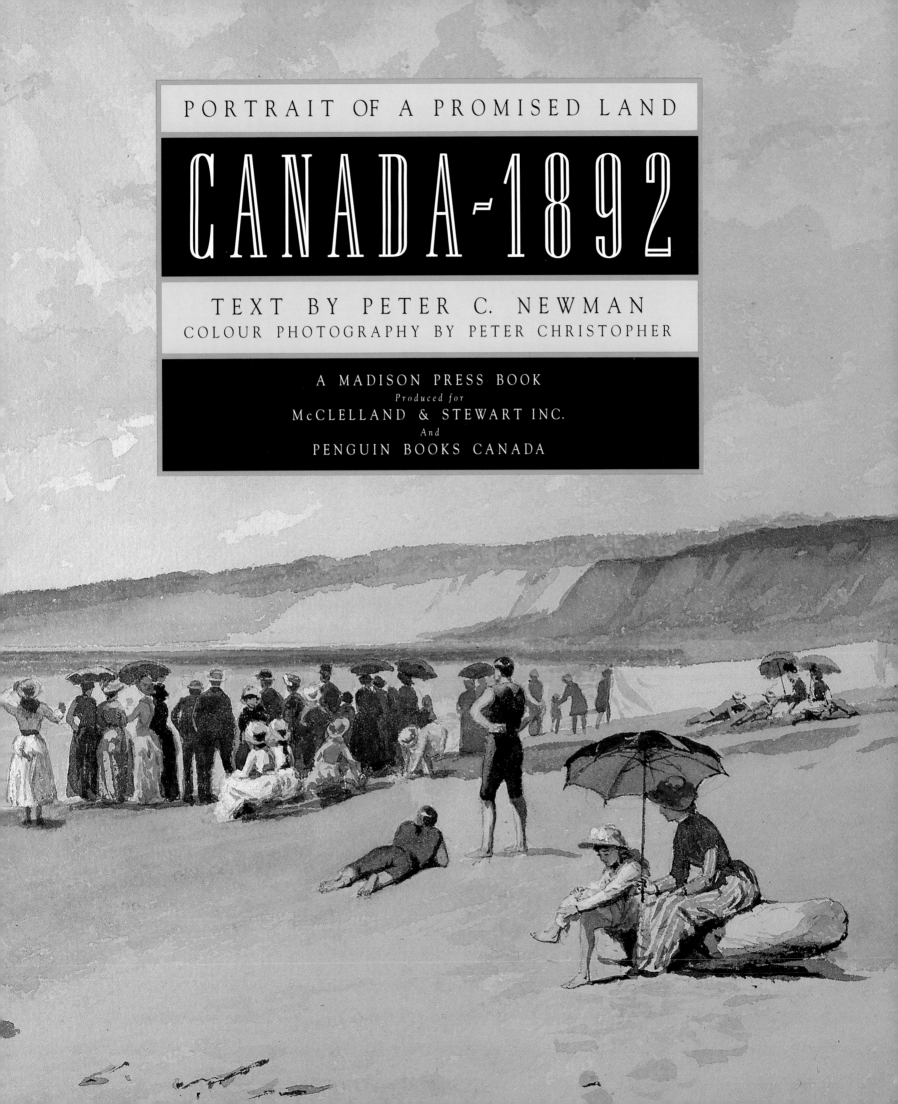

PORTRAIT OF A PROMISED LAND

CANADA - 1892

TEXT BY PETER C. NEWMAN
COLOUR PHOTOGRAPHY BY PETER CHRISTOPHER

A MADISON PRESS BOOK
Produced for
McCLELLAND & STEWART INC.
And
PENGUIN BOOKS CANADA

First published in Canada by

PENGUIN BOOKS CANADA LIMITED
10 Alcorn Avenue, Suite 300, Toronto, Ontario M4V 3B2

and

McCLELLAND & STEWART INC.
The Canadian Publishers
481 University Avenue, Toronto, Ontario M5G 2E9

Canadian Cataloguing in Publication Data

Newman, Peter C., 1929–
  Canada 1892

ISBN 0–670–84575–2

1. Canada—History—1867–1914. I. Title.

FC505.N48 1992   971.05   C92–093101–4
F1033.N48 1992

Produced by Madison Press Books
40 Madison Avenue, Toronto, Ontario, Canada M5R 2S1

Printed in Canada

FOR
KRISTINA,
MY GIFT FROM THE SEA

CONTENTS

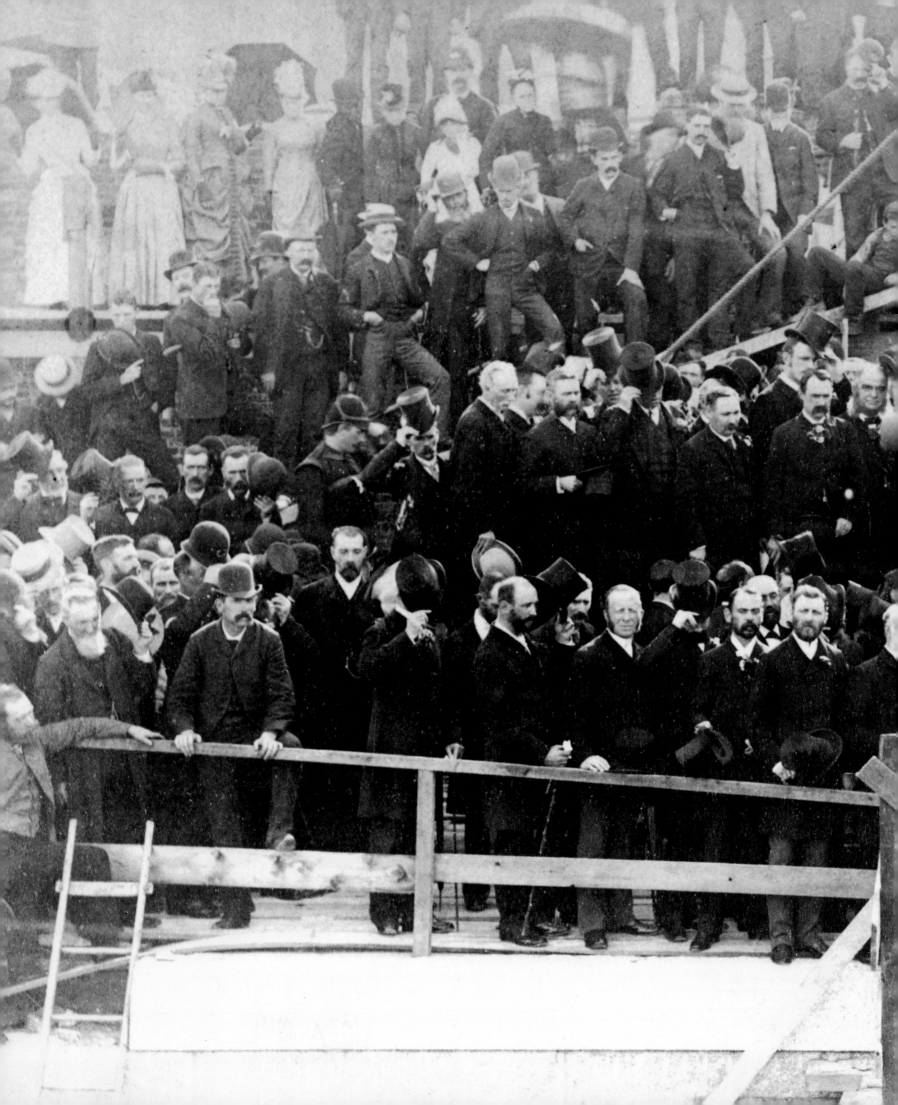

PORTRAIT OF A
PROMISED LAND

A light shines from the
Romanesque tower of
Craigdarroch, the
Dunsmuir family
mansion in Victoria.

CANADA 1892:
PORTRAIT OF A PROMISED LAND

N THE HISTORY OF EVERY COUNTRY THERE COMES A PIVOTAL MOMENT WHEN ITS URBAN future overtakes its rural past. Canada in 1892 was experiencing just such a time. Up till then, the large lone land had seemed little more than a brooding geographical mass, silent and inaccessible, its sparse population laying reluctant claim to the shoulders of its shores, the elbows of its rivers and the laps of its mountains.

But by 1892 the young Dominion had begun the momentous if painful time of its maturing. With the recently completed Canadian Pacific Railway tying the country together, the empty territories were beginning to fill up, and the place names on the map now denoted not just felled trees or dug cellars, but expanding settlements, alive with the noise and sweat of commerce. Villages were growing into towns, towns into cities, and a half-dozen virtual city-states were emerging across the country.

Modern Canadians walking the streets of Montreal or Toronto, Quebec City, Halifax or Victoria in the 1890s would witness a different world from the one they know today. And yet, scattered here and there would be familiar landmarks. Architecturally, 1892 and its period was a significant watershed – some of that era's best buildings became a part of the Canadian heritage. They included Toronto's Old City Hall, York Club and Queen's Park; the Château Frontenac in Quebec City; Windsor Station in Montreal; various buildings in Vancouver's Gastown and the Dunsmuir mansion, Craigdarroch, in Victoria. Such popular period fashions as Richardsonian Romanesque and the Château set the styles for Canada's public and private buildings for many years to come and helped fix the character of the nation's streets.

As the 1890s transformed Canada's physical appearance, turning the still infant Dominion into an urban and industrialized land, other forces were operating on the recently minted Confederation – trends and events that would see bitter conflict within its borders and draw it into five wars beyond them.

"The nineties witnessed the sunset of the Victorian ethic," noted June Callwood in her wonderful history of the period, "the passing of a time when the role and importance of God, the Queen, the flag, duty, honour, virtue and family life were all clearly defined.... It was an era of great contrasts, of chastity and brothels, censorship and pornography.... of crippling poverty and bounteous windfall; tough bosses and violent labour disputes; an age of cesspools and sterilization, plagues and dramatic medical advances; French-English conflict; prairie droughts and booms; gold rushes and emigration; puritanical men and militant women; sporting houses and Klondike hurdy-gurdy girls."

Federal-provincial relations in 1892 proved unusually combative, with Quebec and Ontario fed up with having to subsidize the poorer provinces ("the shreds and patches of Confederation"). The premiers – W.S. Fielding of Nova Scotia, Frederick Peters of Prince Edward Island, A.G. Blair of New Brunswick, de Boucherville and Taillon of Quebec (Honoré Mercier had been dismissed from office but was still fighting),

Oliver Mowat of Ontario, Thomas Greenway of Manitoba and Theodore Davie of British Columbia – were united by one emotion: their outrage with Ottawa's every pronouncement. True to form, the Western premiers were particularly upset about exorbitant freight rates; the Maritimers were demanding higher fishing quotas.

Spurred on by the rulings of the United Kingdom's Judicial Committee of the Privy Council, federal powers were being drastically decentralized, so that most Ottawa initiatives seemed blunted. Economically, times were tough, with Canada suffering its share of a world-wide recession. Industries that had been built up under the high-tariff National Policy (which had kept out most competing American goods) found they couldn't compete and resorted to layoffs and consolidations. The only solution, insiders in both major parties whispered, was "unrestricted reciprocity" (free trade) with the United States.

Always strained, French-English relations were reaching a new low in cordiality. "Between English and French Canada lay a gulf of incomprehension bridged only by the necessities of politics," concluded John Saywell in his study of the 1890s. "Bigotry was widespread, finding outlets in the traditional French-English and Catholic-Protestant conflicts, in hostility to any strangers in the land, and in sharp rivalries among Protestant sects. The tone of the Nineties was rough and discordant." Reflecting that mood, former Quebec premier Pierre Chauveau had observed, "English and French, we climb by a double flight of stairs towards the destinies reserved for us on this continent, without knowing each other, without meeting each other, and without even seeing each other except on the landing of politics."

That "landing of politics" was forever altered in the summer of 1891 by the death of the great improviser, *the* Father of Confederation, Sir John A. Macdonald. Like some magnificent, indestructible lighthouse in a field of puny chimneys, Macdonald was not only Canada's founding prime minister, but the stalwart role model for each of his less worthy successors. With an unerring instinct for his political enemies' jugulars and an uncanny ability to take on whatever ideological colouration each situation demanded, he dominated Canada's post-Confederation scene for more than a quarter of a century. In the process, he turned opportunism and patronage into something close to Canada's state religion, and yet it was his genius to turn his healthy brand of pragmatism into a significant force for nation-building.

Macdonald's impressive achievement of forging a Conservative party out of such anomalous forces as English Canada's fledgling business establishment and Quebec's Catholic hierarchy attested to the reach of his skill. Within Ontario, Tory support came largely from manufacturers happy with the harsh tariffs of Sir John's National Policy. Even though the majority of these industrialists were raging Protestants, they happily joined with the Pope's representatives in French Canada to sit under the umbrella of Macdonald's mildly progressive conservatism, united by their opposition to the forces of liberal secularism which by 1892 were beginning to sweep the country.

Perhaps his attraction as a politician was partly based on the fact that he seemed as vulnerable as the new and still wobbly Dominion itself – barely able to stand on his own feet after repeated bouts with his favourite brand of the demon rum – yet somehow surviving with spirit unbowed. His greatest strength was just being there, personifying survival – his own and his country's.

In the last decade of his life, Macdonald spent his increasingly infrequent sober hours cajoling, bribing and inspiring the voters to follow his winding path to glory. He may have viewed the new world he was

Sir John A. Macdonald in his study. The death of Macdonald on June 6, 1891, left a vacuum in Canadian political life in 1892.

creating through bloodshot eyes, but he governed Canada's awesome chunk of geography with the hard-won wisdom of a man with a million miles on his meter.

By the time the 1891 election rolled around, Macdonald, then in his seventy-seventh year, had spent half a century in the tumbling discontinuity of a political process so crude that those who actually followed its few rules of ethical conduct were judged to be either stupid or senile. Macdonald himself had made so many compromises to keep his country and his party together that he could no longer be sure where he himself stood on any issue.

As he prepared to face the voters one last time, the country had never seemed so troubled and so divided. Nova Scotia had begun to talk secession and in fact had formally voted to leave Confederation. There was dissatisfaction everywhere about everything, so that within twenty-five years of Canada's birth, the Dominion's future appeared less secure than ever.

In the face of such high political risks and while battling his own deteriorating health, Macdonald at the start of the 1891 election looked not so much old as dead, kept going only by increasingly frequent doses of booze, the ravaged topography of his face resembling the weather side of an ancient mountain gully.

There really was no issue other than Macdonald himself, although the Tories were not above attacking Laurier's Liberals as traitors for toying with the idea that Canada join the United States (while themselves secretly trying to negotiate a new brand of reciprocity with Washington). When he asked Governor General Lord Stanley to dissolve Parliament and call an election for March 5, Macdonald penned a public letter that laid out his position: "As for myself, my course is clear. A British subject I was born – a British subject I will die. With my utmost effort, with my last breath, will I oppose the 'veiled treason' which attempts by sordid means and mercenary proffers to lure our people from their allegiance." That statement was widely interpreted precisely for what it was meant to be: not an assertion of imperial support, but a declaration of Canadian patriotism. It worked.

The Canadian Manufacturers' Association swung in behind the old man. Sir William Van Horne, president of the Canadian Pacific Railway, assured Macdonald that "the CPR vote will be practically unanimous" – not surprising given that the CPR had been described as the "Tory Government on Wheels." Macdonald wrapped himself in the Union Jack ("The Old Flag – The Old Policy – The Old Leader") and charged the Liberals with treason for trying "to make Canada the Arctic fringe on the American blanket." Although he was not feeling well enough to do much personal campaigning, whenever he did, his presence caused a sensation. As Macdonald stepped forward at his main Toronto rally ("the familiar long, crooked body half a step behind the famous long crooked nose," as one writer put it) the audience reacted with an emotional sigh that could only be described as an expression of love. "The grand old hero stood there motionless as his heart throbbed within his honoured breast," reported the *Empire*.

Canadians responded appropriately on election night, granting Macdonald a twenty-seven-seat margin – a larger share of the popular vote than he had received in 1887. But the campaign broke what was left of his health. Three months later, on June 6, 1891, he was dead.

Eras end with the passing of each prime minister, but this was something different. Regardless of party loyalty, Canadians mourned Sir John's death as if a family member had been removed from their very firesides.

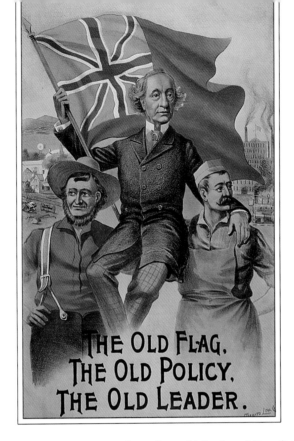

THE OLD FLAG.
THE OLD POLICY.
THE OLD LEADER.

A farmer and a factory worker, representing the two groups who benefited the most from Macdonald's protectionist National Policy, here support the centre-piece of the Tories' 1891 campaign.

Of the many obituaries, none was more moving than that of Macdonald's political opponent, Wilfrid Laurier. "The place of Sir John A. Macdonald in this country was so large and so absorbing," the Liberal leader told the Commons, "that it is almost impossible to conceive that the politics of this country – the fate of this country – will continue without him. His loss overwhelms us.... He now belongs to the ages and it can be said with certainty that the career which has been just closed is one of the most remarkable careers in this century. The life of Sir John A. Macdonald, from the date he entered parliament, is the history of Canada."

As Canadians faced the first year in memory without the Old Chief in power, they wondered what 1892 would bring them. It would be a significant if troubled year for both Canada and the world. In Britain the Liberals under William Gladstone won a slim electoral victory, while Keir Hardie became the first Labour member of Parliament. Bernard Shaw published *Mrs Warren's Profession* and Rudyard Kipling bought out his *Barrack Room Ballads*. In the United States, Democrat Grover Cleveland won the presidency, opposing the McKinley Tariff, which would have hurt Canada. *Vogue* magazine began publishing in New York, and Pittsburgh saw the most violent strike in American labour history as club-wielding Pinkerton men battled strikers at Andrew Carnegie's Homestead works. Russia suffered famine and France went to war against King Behanzin in Africa. In sports, "Gentleman Jim" Corbett defeated John L. Sullivan for the heavyweight championship, while in technology, the diesel engine and the automatic telephone switchboard were perfected.

In Canada that year, Honoré Mercier was acquitted on corruption charges, and poet Pauline Johnson began her public readings. In a still too familiar pattern, two Canadians were on their way to achieving world renown – in the United States. James Naismith would invent basketball while working at the YMCA in Springfield, Massachusetts, and actress Marie Dressler (Leila Koerber of Cobourg, Ontario) made her first appearance on Broadway. Lead, silver and zinc deposits were discovered at Kimberley, British Columbia, and work was underway on the making of the world's biggest cheese (thirteen tons) in Perth, Ontario.

The country's 1892 gross national product was about $460 million, and Canadians had socked away $55 million in savings accounts. But the original post-Confederation dream, which had envisioned a prosperous nation stretching from sea to sea, had yet to come true. The recession would continue to batter industry in central Canada and hurt eastern Canada even more. Fewer than a quarter of a million newcomers had chosen to settle on the western plains. The great wave of immigration that would see 1.5 million Europeans farming Canada's prairies was still a decade away.

The automobile, the movie and the radio – the three inventions most responsible for changing social behaviour early in this century – had yet to be introduced, but life was becoming decidedly easier. Canadians were rapidly getting used to typewriters, central heating, indoor toilets, barbed wire (to keep track of the cows), Linotype machines, kerosene, half-tone newspaper photos, steam-powered threshers and, above all, electric lights, streetcars and telephones. The early phones were treated with a certain degree of suspicion. Phone subscribers felt sure that somehow the talking machines were conveying false information, and for many years after they were introduced, Canadians used telephones mainly to make appointments to visit their friends in person. By 1892 almost every major Canadian city had an electrified streetcar system in operation, but many old-timers were still afraid of electricity. Times changed, and so did Canadians – but warily.

Canadians, then as now, were marked by an ability to endure – to survive a lousy climate and worse politicians. That will has always been a Canadian burden. Concentrating too much on survival, however, often deters imagination and creativity – those intuitive leaps that allow individuals and countries to reach for greatness. Yet survivors are the winners in any game, and it is because Canada's survival is threatened in 1992, as it was in 1892, that the mood and details of what happened in that distant year are significant.

As Canadians head into an uncertain decade, memories of precious times past take on a very special glow, keeping pride alive in our country and ourselves. But folk memories don't reproduce themselves; they must be preserved and sustained.

Anniversaries such as the current celebration of Canada's 125th birthday help reinvent the past in a highly selective way; we decide what to remember and choose what to forget. That presents alternatives for the present and decides priorities for the future.

This book is less a commemoration of an official birthday than a guided tour of the Canada that existed in 1892. That is no prehistoric venture. It is a time as close to us as our grandparents or great-grandparents. This, after all, is a country only four memories old, and history is nothing more, and nothing less, than those memories refined – the record of collective and individual encounters between character and circumstance. If we care to listen, we can still hear the faint echoes of the people who walked our streets, worked our farms and fished our waters a hundred years ago.

Although the great era of immigration would begin a few years later, settlers, in this case American Mormons, were beginning to trickle into the Canadian West by 1892.

NO GILDED AGE

VERY AGE HAS ITS STEREOTYPES, AND THE 1890S WERE NO EXCEPTION. THE ICONS OF THE time were Lillie Langtry and the Prince of Wales, the Vanderbilts and the Astors. It was an age when the American tycoon Jay Gould sent his card to one of the Rothschilds and had it returned with the comment, "Europe is not for sale." It was certainly an age of excess – in architecture, interior decor, dress and spending habits – but Canada was only partially in step with these extravagances.

We had our share of tycoons, but collectively they bore little resemblance to the sophisticated if slightly fading aristocrats of Europe or the slick socialites of the New York 400. While Macdonald's National Policy and the building of the railroads had created a moneyed class centred largely in Montreal, not a single one of its members had been raised in privilege. Donald Smith and George Stephen, the mighty duo who financed the Canadian Pacific Railway, had spent most of their lives in such mundane occupations as trading furs with the natives of Labrador (Smith's main calling) or, in Stephen's case, assisting in his uncle's tiny drapery store in Montreal.

Canada's rich were men and women with the mentality and telescopic outlook of shopkeepers and bankers, bearing the stamp of stiff, duty-bound prudery. Their conscience was equally susceptible to the hope of heaven and fast depreciation write-offs, or the fear of hell. They were Scottish (even if they came from Sweden or Poland) to the marrow of their souls, and whatever their backgrounds or religions, they knew how to parlay endurance of the spirit into earthly salvation.

Whatever his humble origins and his essentially middle-class legacy, the typical Canadian tycoon of the 1890s certainly looked the part. Canada's home-grown robber barons didn't feel properly attired without cane, cigar and morning coat, and they proudly exhibited their great girth, which was taken as the sign of a truly prosperous man. Conspicuous consumption on a regal scale – not to mention conspicuous waste and conspicuous leisure – marked their time.

A highly artificial system of etiquette – a most un-Canadian set of customs – governed nearly all the social transactions of the rich. Their daughters, whose main purpose in life was to capture a socially acceptable (preferably titled) husband, became especially enmeshed in the elaborate pretensions of the etiquette books that listed precise instructions on everything from the length of one's gloves to how to park one's hat and how to descend from a carriage in a ladylike fashion. Only the hostess could shake a guest's hand during "at homes"; guests were allowed merely to salute one another with "a studied inclination of the head, a fleeting smile, and a murmur of the name."

Canada's moneyed classes drank Madeira after dinner and tended to live in pretend-British manor houses peopled by snobbish nannies, nervous maids and patronizing butlers. Interior decor was based on the notion that leaving even one square inch of wall or table space unfilled by clutter constituted bad taste.

Of all the era's status symbols, the most desired by the rich was the private railway car. And since most of their fortunes were based on the railways, it was a natural toy for them to acquire. The cars, as one contemporary writer noted, were "jewel cases on wheels," with crystal chandeliers, furniture upholstered in velvet, and fresh flowers in crystal vases. The decor provided solace for the discomfort of train travel over uneven rail beds, though on some stretches it was impossible to bathe properly because the water kept slopping out of the coaches' tubs. Fortunately there was always plenty of soothing champagne on hand to smooth out the ride.

Despite their profoundly superior airs, most of these commercial aristocrats were insecure in their *nouveau riche* homes and finery. But they were damned if they were going to give up one gold-plated water-basin tap or one silk collar. In fact, they genuinely believed that their lavish spending habits constituted a patriotic act. "Were the wealthier citizens of Montreal to shut down upon spending their incomes freely," opined the local *Journal of Commerce*, "were they to take to heart the outcry against the extravagances of the rich, the effect would be seriously disastrous to the business of the city, and none would suffer so much as the industrial classes into whose pockets there ultimately comes the vast bulk of the money spent by the wealthy. Were all men to turn into misers, commerce would be blighted, and civilization would recede."

The rich saw themselves as instruments of the national will; and they were convinced that their personal monetary success and the nation's expanding destiny were inextricably linked. Their operational code was encapsulated in the slogan "God helps those who help themselves," and they helped themselves amply, comfortable in their faith that since it was clearly God's design that the virtuous become wealthy, to gain riches meant qualifying for divine sanction.

The fountainhead of most of this gusher of new money was the invention of stock corporations. Instead of the former personal partnerships which limited profits to more or less reasonable limits, the inauguration of stock markets meant that shares could be manipulated to gain control over enormous capital pools with minimum investments. For example, George Stephen, Donald Smith and three of the other founding partners in the Canadian Pacific

Although they liked to dress their children as miniature adults, the Victorian rich were among the first to view childhood as a state separate from the adult world. Children were to be protected in nanny-run nurseries and private schools, emerging after a long process as graceful young adults.

Railway, borrowed $250,000 and invested it in the bankrupt St Paul, Minneapolis and Manitoba Railway, which after a decade of stock manipulation yielded them $600 million. Some 1,300 railroads were eventually chartered in Canada. Nearly every one, thanks to stock speculation, became the source of a family fortune, even if very few tracks were actually laid and even fewer trains ever got to use them.

The age of railway building and manipulation diluted the restraints of the pioneer ethic at a time when governments did not yet see intervention in the market as part of their job. The creed of allowing only the fittest and fastest to survive was widely accepted, with the rich and powerful being admired and even revered while the poor and jobless were accused of sloth, incompetence and moral ineptitude.

Reflecting this Darwinian outlook, business in the 1890s suffered from about as many constraints as piracy on the high seas three centuries earlier. Labour unions were small and nearly powerless; there was no income tax; Ottawa's tariff and transportation policies were tailored specifically to help big business turn more profit; and environmental and safety codes had yet to be invented. Although he was writing about the United States, Mark Twain's musings about the free enterprise system applied equally across the border. "What is the chief end of man?" he asked, using the words memorized in Protestant Sunday schools for generations, then gave his own cynical answer, "To get rich. In what way? Dishonestly if he can; honestly if he must. Who is God, the one only and true? Money is God. Gold and Greenbacks and stock – father, son, and the ghost of the same – three persons in one; these are the true and only God."

By the summer of 1892 the amount of chartered bank notes in circulation was the highest in the history of the country. In one fairly typical month – November of 1892 – $39,318,218 changed hands. The gross value of Canadian manufacturing rose from $221 million to $370 million during the two decades preceding 1892 (a jump of sixty-seven percent), but weaker firms were being absorbed by stronger rivals, while the slow-down of major railway construction, a looming recession, and most of all, fierce competition, made the short-term outlook bleak. "Men go into business to earn a living," patiently explained the *Canadian Grocer*, then the country's leading trade journal. "There are often circumstances which seriously interfere with their ability to do so. The greatest of these is competition."

The agony of competition was something no humble employee could ever hope to understand. "His hours of labour are fixed, and his work is of a routine nature, requiring very little thought or care, except that necessary to the faithful performance of his duties," the *Grocer* editorialized. "He knows just how much he is making, and when his day's work is done he can lay aside all care without fret or worry. But with his employer it is quite different. With him it is constant, unceasing work, and his mind can never be entirely free from his business cares. Not for a moment can he rest."

In order to take the sting out of commercial rivalry, firms attempted various forms of combines and monopolies; competition was too destructive to be allowed to exist. Ottawa did almost nothing to prevent such restrictive trade practices, allowing industries to form guilds, associations, trusts and pools and to amalgamate without restraint – to do anything, in short, as long as they didn't frighten the horses.

Thus were perpetuated and expanded the youthful Dominion's business dynasties: the Dunsmuirs in British Columbia; the Burns family in what would become Alberta; the Richardsons in Winnipeg; the Eatons and Masseys in Toronto; and the Molsons in Montreal. These great family firms became so powerful that they

With industrialization and mass production came advertising. Selling techniques in the 1890s ranged from colourful posters, such as the one (left) for the Acadia Powder Company, to enticing guarantees such as that for Wilson's Fly Pads (bottom right). Another popular advertising medium were trade cards, small colour cards often handed out in the street. These advertised anything from cigars (bottom middle) to trade cards themselves (bottom left).

operated almost outside normal business channels. When John H.R. Molson (a grandchild of that brewing dynasty's founder) lay dying in 1897, he dictated a telling message to his heirs. "The Molson family," he decreed, "has maintained and preserved its position and influence by steady, patient industry, and every member should be a real worker and not rely upon what it has been.... Your private lives should be pure. Make no compromise with vice, be able to say no in a firm manner. Character is the real test of manhood."

Canada's best-known merchant adventurer in 1892 was probably Sir Casimir Stanislaus Gzowski, an engineer and militia officer born in St Petersburg, Russia. The son of an army officer who was a member of the minor Polish nobility, Gzowski immigrated to the United States in 1834. He studied law before switching to engineering and helped build much of Pennsylvania's original canal and railway infrastructure. Eight years after he arrived in America, Gzowski moved north into Canada, and became superintendent of public works for the Province of Canada. He improved Yonge Street up to Lake Simcoe, built several harbours and eventually got into railway construction, a move that put him in touch with the country's moneyed classes.

For the next four decades Gzowski was one of Canada's shrewdest and busiest contractors, occasionally cutting corners but never getting caught. With age came social legitimacy. He changed his official occupation on the census forms from contractor to gentleman and moved into a massive brick house on Toronto's Bathurst Street, surrounded by conservatories, stables and a guest lodge. Having become a staunch Anglican, he tiptoed into Toronto's highest social ranks and devoted himself to good causes.

Gzowski resolutely stayed out of partisan politics, or more precisely, he helped John A. Macdonald's Tories federally and Oliver Mowat's Liberals provincially. Eventually knighted and promoted to a colonel in the militia, he became Canada's favourite Grand Old Man – an unexpected honour for a Polish immigrant, no matter how capable, ambitious or cultured.

Few of the rich and powerful in the 1890s suffered from an enlarged social conscience, but there were enough philanthropists among them (who believed it was cheaper to bestow good works than good wages) to provide at least some help to the poor. They paid their employees as little as possible and kept working conditions at a barely tolerable level, ever mindful of Adam Smith's advice that "parsimony, and not industry, is the immediate cause of the increase of capital," but they also believed in having a "decent lustre" shed on their wealth. That meant caring – or at least appearing to care – for the poor. "Charities were the incumbencies of the wealthy families," wrote C.L. Burton, then the head of Robert Simpson's. "It was part of the dignity and office of wealth to support a charity. The older established families had what amounted to personal charitable institutions, which they supported and governed. Woe betide any upstart who trespassed or tried to trespass upon one of these essentially private charities."

But charity has a cold heart, especially when it depends on the whims of the rich. As more and more workers joined larger and larger companies, unions sprang up to protect employees' rights. The Canadian organized labour movement had started among the bakers of Victoria and the printers of New Brunswick in the late 1850s, and the Trades Union Act of 1873 had encouraged its spread. At first, for their own protection, unionists created what amounted to secret societies, communicating by confidential handshakes and taking part in closed meetings under an oath of silence. Among organized labour's initial demands were free compulsory education, eight-hour days and six-day weeks, minimum living wages, prohibition of child labour, abolition of the Senate, and the exclusion from Canada of Orientals.

The most successful movement was the Knights of Labour, whose militant leaders, some of them imported Americans, made management back down in several touchy situations. But as often as not, militia regiments (and even, in one Vancouver Island dispute in the Dunsmuir coal mines, a Royal Navy warship) were use to quell the strikers. Management won nearly every strike, but the *Canadian Manufacturer* still complained that "the tyranny of trades-unionism is simply damnable."

Yet the winds of change had begun to blow. No matter how grand the fortresses of established wealth and power might be, their ramparts had been breached, and nothing would be the same again.

Still, the 1890s was a decade of extravagant contrasts, and nowhere was this more evident than in the difference between the monstrous wealth of the mercantile classes and the debasing want of the poorest urban Canadians. Unlike today, the poor were provided with no safety nets; worse, their condition was thought to be a sign of their own weakness of character. What little help municipal governments provided was limited to "public recreation" facilities and "homes for the feeble minded." The poor were thought to be either lazy or dissolute by nature, so that any help given them was bound to be wasted.

The poor lived – or rather existed – in slums of tar-paper shacks that rented for six dollars a month with open-pit sewers and contaminated drinking water. They had access to few full-time jobs, were permanently in debt and only managed to scrape by because every member of the family toiled from sun-up to sunset at whatever work was available. Their ranks were multiplied by a constant influx from the country.

Generally, the rich dealt with the plight of the poor by not thinking about it. Yet small public flashes of agony did surface. There was the case of a Mrs Agnes Warren, who lived at the gypsy camp in East Toronto, for example. Charged with shoplifting a can of salmon to feed her child, she was reported as having had "seven fits" in court when she was sentenced to thirty days, because she would be separated from her little girl, who could not fend for herself. The Saint-Alexis de Montréal orphanage reported that only one percent of its inhabitants actually had no parents; the rest of the children were placed there by their mothers and fathers because there seemed no other way to keep them fed.

In December 1886, Ottawa appointed a royal commission to consider the relationship between labour and capital in Canada. Having heard firsthand testimony across the country on just how bad working conditions really were, the commissioners produced an enlightened report full of progressive suggestions. The government ignored them all (except the least important, which called for the establishment of Labour Day as a national holiday), but the commission's hearings at least provided a snapshot of the grim reality on the other side of the social ledger.

To help stave off hunger, many of the urban poor raised animals in their backyards; according to one calculation, as many as twenty percent of the families in Montreal's notorious Griffintown kept pigs and cows, which did little to improve local sanitation. The street was the children's playground and frequently their workplace, where they could earn money begging, or peddling newspapers or themselves. There were many cases of mothers and daughters working together as prostitutes.

Without doubt, child labour was the worst evil of the age. The introduction of modern machinery in factories meant that persistence rather than true skill was required for most routine jobs, and low-paid children seemed the ideal work force. Working conditions were primeval. This was how the commission described a typical cigar factory: "In stifling air foul with odors of tobacco, machine oil, perspiration and a thousand other evil-smelling substances, are seated the slaves of the leaf. Young and old, women and men, boys and girls, from seven o'clock in the morning to six o'clock at night, with one short hour for dinner, they toil for three dollars a week, and sometimes two. There are no toilet appliances, no fire escapes, no facilities for ventilation: there is nothing but work and a brutal foreman to enforce it." In clothing factories, leaky gas irons turned work-rooms

For many children of the poor, such as this barefoot youngster on Quebec's Breakneck Steps, the street was their only playground. (Inset) Needy

Toronto children being treated to a day at the Exhibition in 1892 by the Fresh Air Fund, a charity founded by journalist J.J. Kelso to aid the children of the poor.

into literal sweat-shops, the steam so thick sometimes that workers could hardly see one another. One employee at a Cornwall mill testified that "in ten or eleven years a good able-bodied man will be like a broken down streetcar horse." The adults succumbed to tuberculosis, while diphtheria claimed the children.

Quebec's 1890 Factory Act tried to limit hiring to boys over fourteen and girls over fifteen, but birth certificates were readily falsified. One father was so desperate for the income his three children could earn that the birth certificates he produced for them showed they were all born in the same year. Some unscrupulous bosses took on unpaid youngsters in so-called apprentice schemes, fired them when their apprenticeships were up, and then enlisted a new group of "volunteers." Ottawa's royal commission discovered that children as young as ten were working sixty-hour weeks in manufacturing (and seventy-two hours in such service occupations as shoeshine boys or domestics) and that they were paid as little as $1.50 a week – one-sixth the adult wage. In Cape Breton the commissioners found many examples of ten-year-old boys working in the coal pits.

Such worthy organizations as the Salvation Army and the Grey Nuns did their best, but the problems were just too overwhelming, and no one in an official position to help seemed inclined to do so. John Joseph Kelso, a police reporter for the Toronto *World*, was horrified to witness children as young as six being sentenced to jail for stealing life's necessities. He was also deeply moved by the tragedy of a nine-year-old prostitute who was earning ten cents per customer. When he read about a group collecting funds to prevent cruelty to horses, Kelso attended their meeting, persuaded them to give human misery a priority and founded the Children's Aid Society and Fresh Air Fund, becoming one of Toronto's first full-time social reformers.

By 1892 most provinces had started to adopt legislation making primary school attendance compulsory, which would eventually help correct some of the worst excesses of child labour. This wasn't the case for that other mode of merciless labour exploitation: domestic piece-work. With pay rates set at the very margin of their endurance, the women who subsisted on piece-work had to collect and carry home bundles of cloth, do the necessary work, then wait for a subcontractor to collect the finished garments. A skilled seamstress could make a boy's double-breasted overcoat, complete with three buttonholes and a half-belt at the back, for fourteen cents. Underwear contractors paid forty-eight cents per dozen, or four cents a piece.

It was not surprising that the most popular place to be, if you lived in the poor sections of town, was the local tavern. Herbert Brown Ames, the author of *The City Below the Hill*, an early account of poverty in Montreal, counted the number of drinking establishments in that city's working quarter – 105 saloons and 78 grocery shops that sold liquor, which came to one booze outlet for every thirty-three families. The same was true on the western frontier, where it was not uncommon for a tiny mining settlement to boast one saloon for every dozen stuporous citizens. Vancouver had twenty-nine breweries for a population of 25,000, and Canadians were quaffing beer at the rate of four gallons per capita annually.

It was the age of long, polished mahogany bars, brass spittoons and understanding bartenders with sly moustaches and pawnbrokers' eyes. Under the Canada Temperance Act, passed in 1878, any Canadian municipality had the right to declare itself dry. In those places that bothered to do so, it just meant that liquor was consumed in secret, becoming an even more tantalizing commodity. Efforts to curb the runaway consumption of alcohol spawned active temperance organizations that saw "the demon rum" not only as undermining the boozers' health but interfering with the sanctity of family life. The lecture circuits became clogged with crusaders like Thomas Doutney, who advertised himself as an "Ex-liquor Dealer and Reformed Inebriate" and promised to stage a stirring spectacle consisting of "Scores Signing the Pledge! Spicy Talks! and Delineations of Bar-room Characters, with dialect peculiar to each."

Unfortunately for their cause, the temperance and prohibition crusaders so overstated their case that its impact was blunted. One 1892 pamphlet claimed that intemperance was hereditary and quoted the following extract from something called the Department of Heredity and Hygiene: "Recently a friend of mine was urging a boy two [sic] years of age to join the Band of Hope, when he startled her by saying, 'You don't know what you are asking of me. Never drink any more liquor? I love it better than my life, I could not live without it.' Think you that was an acquired taste with that child? No, no; his parents are responsible for it. 'A corrupt tree cannot bring forth good fruit.'"

Some Canadians didn't require the stigma of alcohol to be treated in an inferior and shoddy way. Indians and other minority groups were treated with just as little respect. Anglo-conformity remained the prime virtue, and those who were different found themselves condemned for it. Blacks were nicknamed "Coons," "Niggers" or "Darkies"; Chinese "Chinks"; Jews "Yids"; and Quebecers "Frogs."

Canada, then, was still uncertain about itself, about what it meant to be a Canadian. And to be anything but rich and Anglo-Saxon meant being permanently an outsider.

With its racy painting over the bar, conveniently placed spittoon and congenial company, the Hoffman House in Rossland, B.C., epitomized the saloons of the period.

WHAT WAS NEW AND FASCINATING ABOUT LIFE IN THE 1890s WAS THAT FOR THE FIRST TIME there was an opportunity for most people to enjoy leisure. More Canadians had money to spend, and more of them were living in urban areas where mass entertainments were available to everyone. The growing production of books and sports equipment brought people new choices, and Canada's railways fostered the organization of national touring companies that filled local theatres and music halls.

But the one leisure activity that overshadowed all others was cycling. The bicycle, which was as much a sociological as a sporting phenomenon, changed Canada.

The country went bicycle-mad. Here was the affordable vehicle that could endow city dwellers with mobility and freedom. Not only that. It was socially unrestricted, so that a washerwoman might find herself riding beside a bank manager, while a chimney sweep could be pumping his pedals alongside the mayor's wife.

Women took to cycling most enthusiastically because it gave them the freedom to travel unescorted wherever they wished and, most important, gave them the chance to wear more sensible, less constricting clothes such as divided skirts, breeches and other items (known as "bifurcated nether garments") that allowed

freer body movement. The switch in fashion, especially to bloomers, was not met with universal acclaim. "The female who wears them is a fright," harrumphed *Saturday Night*. "The bloomers have revealed the most shapeless lot of legs ever seen outside a butcher shop."

Invented in England, the bicycle took the place of earlier bone-shakers like the penny farthing, substituting two wheels of equal size and propelled by a pedal-powered chain drive. Its simplicity and the use of pneumatic tires made riding not only safe but comfortable. Bicycle academies sprang up in every community to teach the subtleties of the sport, while local and national bicycle clubs staged races, rallies and tours. Annual exhibitions introducing the new models were mobbed. The Dunlop Trophy Race, held at Toronto's Woodbine Stadium, drew 12,000 spectators.

Like any great innovation, the bicycle had its critics. The *Whitby Chronicle* attacked out-of-town cyclists with their "horse talk, loud body sweat and road perfume." The churches, faced with near-empty pews on sunny Sundays as their congregations went off bicycling, saw the contraptions as instruments of the devil. "You can not serve God and skylark on a bicycle," decreed the Reverend Asa Blackburn.

But nothing could reverse the spiritual freedom that had unexpectedly been granted Canadian city dwellers. More than any other influence, the two-wheelers undermined Victorian priggishness and shattered social barriers.

At the same time that Canadians were winging along the roads in a celebration of two-wheeled freedom, there were stirrings in the country's soul as the first faint glimmerings of a Canadian culture began to

For cyclists like these visiting Aylmer, Quebec, on a day trip from Ottawa, the bicycle represented a new freedom and mobility.

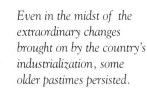

appear. In the theatre, the first Canadian acting companies launched coast-to-coast tours, although the theatre of the nineties was not a terribly high-brow affair. Most of the successful stage shows were overblown "mellerdramas" with elaborate sets, ostentatious costumes, vaudeville subtlety and farcical scripts. Their plot lines seldom touched on social or political issues, but they certainly answered the prayer of the *Globe*'s theatre critic who wrote in 1892, "This we demand: the worthy must be rewarded and the villain punished." No suggestion of lewdness, however gentle, was allowed, and even parts of Shakespeare's *As You Like It* were censored.

Not that audiences seemed to mind. There appeared to be a direct correlation between a play's "wholesomeness" and its popularity, with wholesomeness being defined by how often the stainless hero – ever the macho saint – rescued the rotating series of whimpering maidens and how many times he triumphed over the squirming villain, ever ready to meet his just deserts. To remove any lingering doubt about whom to root for, the villain often wore a black hat and swirling black cape, and ominously twirled the ends of his moustache for a menacing effect.

Vaudeville was another popular theatrical form, as were the concerts (usually played on outdoor stages lit by gas torches) that were as much spectacle as music. These could feature heavenly choirs (occasionally fitted with papier mâché angel wings), instrumental soloists (one favourite was a high-note trumpeter who played while balancing atop a trapeze on one foot) and, inevitably, a clutch of "gifted" local ladies who "obliged" the master of ceremonies by warbling interminably into the night. There were also travelling medicine shows (really small circuses), P.T. Barnum's nomadic collection of caged animals and human freaks, and Buffalo Bill Cody's fading Wild West extravaganza. Competition among these travelling shows was fierce. Circus promoters frequently sabotaged their rivals' wagons and occasionally even burned bridges behind them to beat their competitors to a county fair.

Writing was a more sedate occupation, but only slightly so. Performing authors such as Pauline Johnson toured the same seedy "grand opera houses" as the stage companies, reciting their works in dramatic dress and vibrant cadence.

Contemporary fiction was dominated by plots similar to those found in popular theatre – typically tales of virginal heroines who were exposed to every imaginable wickedness, only to be rescued by the vapid hero who then rode off into the sunset in search of yet another maiden to deliver from evil. At a more literary level, several Canadians were beginning to earn national reputations. Some of the more widely read writers included Archibald Lampman, Duncan Campbell Scott (a poet who became head of Ottawa's Indian Affairs branch), novelist Sara Jeannette Duncan, poet Bliss Carman, and Sir Charles G.D. Roberts (the first Canadian writer to be knighted).

More than a thousand magazines were being published in Canada. Foremost among them was *Saturday Night*, edited by Edmund Sheppard, who had trained as a minister in rural Ontario, but spent his youth in the wilds of frontier Texas driving stage-coaches and punching cattle. P.D. Ross of the *Ottawa Journal* and John S. Willison of the Toronto *Globe* were the leading editorialists of the day, while Joseph "Holy Joe" Atkinson had begun the process of turning the *Toronto Star* (founded in November 1892) into the populist newspaper that would soon boast the country's largest circulation. The nineties were a time when newspapers became vehicles of popular entertainment, their editors and publishers fighting hard to gain readers and advertisers.

With the Current
by William Raphael.
The summer idyll
depicted here was a
departure for the
Montreal artist,
who usually painted
urban scenes.

Of the dozen or so prominent visual artists active in 1892, few have survived with enlarged posthumous reputations, but their works provide pleasant images of the period. They include Lucius O'Brien (who produced the first views of the Rockies as seen from the railway); George Reid (an academic artist whose brooding *Mortgaging the Homestead* was adapted as a poster by both the Grits and the Tories in their 1891 campaigns); Frederic Marlett Bell-Smith (whose *Lights of a City Street* graces the cover of this book and who was granted the honour of painting Queen Victoria in 1895); Homer Watson (labelled by Oscar Wilde as "the Canadian Constable" and probably the best artist of the time); William Raphael (Canada's first major Jewish painter, who specialized in Montreal urban scenes); Horatio Walker (who concentrated on rural Quebec, especially portraits of the "jolly habitant" school); Robert Harris (a Prince Edward Islander who had painted the Fathers of Confederation); Paul Peel (who before his death in 1892 had been known for his sentimental paintings of children); Ozias Leduc (essentially a religious painter); and Edmond Dyonnet (who also had a strong reputation as a teacher).

The most interesting thinker of the day was Goldwin Smith, a graduate of Eton and Oxford, where he later taught modern history and became an ardent supporter of Manchester Liberalism, a *laissez-faire* doctrine that would today be considered extremely right wing. In 1871 he settled in Toronto and began writing on Canadian topics, advocating the assimilation of the French-Canadian culture and the Jewish race by the muscular expansion of Anglo-Saxon civilization. Smith was also an obdurate enemy of female emancipation. "Once women enter the labor market," he wrote, "they will introduce conflict into the domestic scene. If

woman demands equality, she will have to resign privilege; she can not be at once the partner and the competitor of man."

Smith's greatest impact came with the 1891 publication of *Canada and the Canadian Question*, in which he advocated that Canada become "the Scotland of North America" and join the United States. His glib conclusions were based on some genuine insights into the Canadian character and condition, and on his reading of the country as being held together not by the natural bonds of geography, race, language or economics, but by political corruption and the vested interests of protected manufacturers. "Though his analysis and conclusion were rooted in the circumstance of the time," the modern Canadian historian Carl Berger has noted, "Smith's book transcends its immediate origins to become one of the most effective and challenging critiques of Canada ever penned. It is an enormously illuminating series of impressions with sparkling insights into Canada's social history, political practices, cultural life and the ambiguities of her economic growth."

Canada in the nineties could field an impressive roster of artists in a variety of fields. But the country was then – as it still is – a difficult place to practise one's own culture. Mentally if no longer constitutionally, Canadians still regarded themselves as colonials, pale imitations of their British mentors and overlords and capable of producing little of worth.

In Britain itself, Queen Victoria sat confidently on her throne, but the women of her empire, like children and idiots, exercised few rights, could seize even fewer opportunities and like the off-stage voices in Shakespeare's plays, were present without making much individual imprint.

Mortgaging the Homestead *by George Reid. Reid's painting poignantly captured the hardships faced by many farmers during the depression of the early nineties.*

*A farm woman in rural
Quebec bakes bread
in an outdoor clay
oven as captured in this
photograph from the
William Notman studio.*

Canada in 1892 seemed to be a land of expanding possibilities, but women's options had actually narrowed. In the preceding generation, when rural life prevailed, they had been essential partners, helping to clear the land, sewing clothes, churning butter, making candles and quilts, and often acting as the family doctor, minister and teacher. With Canada's urbanization and industrialization, however, the pattern changed. In the new cities and towns, men went outside the home to work and a woman's status declined from required colleague to housewife and consumer – buying what she needed instead of producing it.

Women had more time in the nineties than in pioneer years, but fewer outlets for their energy. The jobs that existed were mainly drudgery, with some of the higher callings – teaching and nursing, midwifery and being a nanny – almost exclusively occupied by spinsters. Post-elementary school education for women was limited mainly to "the polite arts," which meant anything that was neither practical nor controversial. The daughters of the well-connected families were beginning to attend university, but there they came up against the bizarre notion that gentlewomen, being such "frail vessels," were too pure to be subjected to life's realities. Far worse, too much "brain work" would interfere with their child-bearing potential. As a popular sex manual of the time put it, "Girls who are natural and would like to be well married, would do well to avoid education, remembering that the personal advantage to the highly educated woman impairs her usefulness as a mother." The same manual also maintained that men were, by nature, smarter than women.

On a more progressive note, a therapist named F.B. Meyer held that no permanent damage would be caused by allowing women access to certain of the more respectable news sheets. "How still she will sit if the newspaper article is read to her!" he rhapsodized. "How eagerly she will strain her attention to understand! What a thrill of joy it will cause afterwards as she reviews the conversation, to realize that her husband thought her worthy to share in his best thoughts!"

However funny such nonsense seems now, there was a serious side to women's assumed inferiority. With marriage they gave up their legal rights. They could not own property, and their husbands could punish them almost at will. In return, they were saved from the most dreaded of social fates, becoming an "old maid" – doomed to live out their lives with condescending relatives or alone and, all too frequently, in poverty.

The idealized virtues of late Victorian times were respectability and gentility, which for wives translated into inordinate doses of modesty, piety and submissiveness to husband-providers. That must have caused overwhelming psychological, economic and sexual frustration, yet if the tears were there, they were spent in private. Few accounts survive to indicate the intensity of women's blighted hopes.

The tiny band of feminists active at the time kept insisting that their sisters would not lose their womanly qualities by doing men's work. Yet in the process, they perpetuated the myth that to be female was to be more pure and less coarse or selfish than the male of the species. Few activists seemed ready to tackle the double standard that allowed men to be "rough and naughty," while women were supposed to bat their eyelashes and pretend they were half-wits.

Being a housewife meant looking after one's husband, hearth and children. Wifely devotion was demonstrated through tables groaning under quantities of food (fat was a sign of affluence) that had little to do with balanced nutrition. The emphasis of menus seemed to be on sugar (the per capita consumption in 1892 was forty-two pounds) and tea (eighteen pounds).

Hamilton's Julia Arthur was one of a number of Canadian actresses in the late nineteenth century who achieved international success. She was ultimately hailed as the "Sarah Bernhardt of the American Stage."

Domestic troubles were frequent but divorce was rare. It was thought to be far better to keep families intact, however unhappily, than to chance legal separation. A joke typical of the era portrayed an unhappy husband telling his wife that he was making out his will and giving her the right to remarry, "because I can be assured there will be at least one person who will daily mourn my passing."

Getting married in the first place was no easy undertaking. The rituals of courtship were severely circumscribed. Chaperones, usually married aunts or maiden cousins, constantly accompanied young ladies out with their swains, and even engaged couples could not appear in public without the moral protection of an accompanying convoy. While the intense prudery of puritanism had slowly retreated – virtue having increasingly become a matter of appearance – sexual mores remained sanctimoniously frigid. The Puritans had condemned sexual indulgence because, like all worldly pleasures, it was vile and guaranteed eternal damnation; Victorians decried the same sin because it might hurt one's reputation. Misunderstanding about normal sexual functions was rampant, even among otherwise qualified sources. *Lancet*, the authoritative British medical journal, published an academic paper detailing why women by nature could not enjoy sex, unless they were prostitutes.

Women's fashion reflected the closed sexual attitudes of the time, with "choker" necklines, tight-laced bodices, bustles, and skirts tight at the hips and flaring to the ground, while hair was piled high and pinned over false pieces. The richer the wearer, the more awkward the costume, with the clothes of affluent women being so designed as to make even the simplest physical labour almost impossible. There was also an element of beauty by impairment – the more awkward a dress, the more it encouraged protectiveness from men.

Those women who did work outside the home ran up against discrimination in terms both of the fields open to them and the salaries they could earn. Male urban teachers in Canada averaged an annual $776 in 1892; women teachers received $358. The occasional outstanding woman did break into a male profession, but this was very much the exception. Canada's first woman lawyer was Clara Brett Martin of Toronto, who actually was not admitted as a student at law until 1893. Sara Jeannette Duncan, a schoolteacher who later became Canada's first woman parliamentary correspondent and then a novelist, had to start her career writing for the Toronto *Globe* and the *Washington Post* under the *nom de plume* of Garth Grafton. Winnipeg's Cora Hind, who became the first female journalist in western Canada, had to work for years as a stenographer before being hired on by the *Free Press* as an agricultural reporter. Augusta Stowe Gullen, the first woman in Canada to practise medicine legally, almost quit her training in disgust when harassing male colleagues made her studies all but impossible.

About the only profession where women flourished was the stage. Such stars as Cobourg's Marie Dressler, Julia Arthur of Hamilton, Louise Beaudet of Montreal, Ethel Mollison of Saint John, Margaret Anglin of Ottawa, Caroline Miskell of Toronto, Margaret Mather of Tilbury, Ontario, and May Irwin of Whitby, Ontario, made their fortunes acting and singing internationally.

The women who came to maturity in 1892 faced a world still hostile to their aspirations, but there was just enough reform in the wind to promise them a better and more interesting life in the near future.

THE RELUCTANT
PRIME MINISTERS

**I**N THE WAKE OF SIR JOHN A. MACDONALD, CANADIAN POLITICS WALLOWED IN AN UNEASY calm. The old chief was gone and there was no one to take his place. Meanwhile, restless currents rippled and ebbed just below the surface. Although neither the Conservatives nor their Liberal opponents knew it, 1892 provided the issue that would ultimately destroy Macdonald's party and usher in the man who would lead Canada into the twentieth century.

Macdonald's natural heir should have been Sir Charles Tupper, a man who had served as the prime minister's partner in all the important battles: forging Confederation, building the Canadian Pacific Railway, implementing the National Policy and fighting against unrestricted reciprocity with the United States. But at the time of Macdonald's death, Tupper was comfortably settled as Canadian high commissioner to the United Kingdom. He had no seat in Parliament and expressed little enthusiasm for a return to the political wars.

Among the candidates available for the job, Macdonald's personal preference was John Thompson, the former Nova Scotia premier whom he had called "the greatest of all my discoveries." But Thompson was a Catholic (and, worse, a convert), which made him unacceptable to most Ontario Tories. He had also defended Riel's execution, which made him equally unpopular in the Quebec caucus.

The improbable compromise candidate was John Joseph Caldwell Abbott, the most reluctant and least active prime minister in Canadian history. A pooped senator of seventy by the time he became Conservative party leader, Abbott had made his fortune as chief legal adviser to the Canadian Pacific Railway, during both Sir Hugh Allan's initial try at building it and its actual construction by the Smith-Stephen syndicate. He spent most of thirty years as the Tory member for Argenteuil and was appointed to the Senate in 1887, the same year he was elected mayor of Montreal. He didn't seem to do very much in either office, concentrating instead on cultivating orchids at his estate at Senneville on the west end of Montreal Island, as well as playing his favourite games – whist and cribbage. Described as a "caretaker," Abbott was chosen as prime minister because, as he modestly put it, "I was not particularly obnoxious to anybody."

"I hate politics, and what are considered their appropriate methods," he frankly admitted. "I hate notoriety, public meetings, public speeches, caucuses, and every thing that I know of that is apparently the necessary incident of politics – except doing public work to the best of my ability. Why should I go where doing honest work will only make me hated and my ministry unpopular; and where I can only gain reputation and credit by practicing arts which I detest, to acquire popularity?" From the beginning of his tenure, Abbott found it impossible to deal with the many pleaders who came to Ottawa on behalf of their ridings to present petitions for every imaginable cause and project. "If it were not for the deputations wanting money and lands, and the people wanting situation and plunder, I should get on pretty well," he confided to his diary – ignoring the fact

that taking care of such concerns was precisely how Macdonald had built and maintained the Conservatives' powerful party machine.

The only condition Abbott made before becoming Tory leader was that Thompson, who had served as Macdonald's minister of justice, become government leader in the House of Commons. Thompson accepted, but refused to honour Abbott's request that he occupy Macdonald's former parliamentary seat. It stayed unused, like some superstar's hockey sweater, its emptiness loudly proclaiming the loss of its one-time occupant.

By November 24, 1892, only seventeen months after taking office, Abbott could stand the strain no longer and resigned, recommending that Thompson succeed him. This time the Nova Scotia politician agreed, and he was sworn into office on December 7. Protestants who accepted posts in Thompson's cabinet received hate mail accusing them of being dupes of the Jesuits, though some of the furore died down when Thompson appointed a hard-bitten Grand Master of the Orange Order of British North America as controller of customs.

A vibrant forty-eight when he took power, Thompson sported woolly sideburns reaching almost to his massive jaw. He tended to fat (his favourite form of exercise was being rowed down the Rideau Canal), but there was nothing flabby about his thought processes. Frugal and painfully honest, Thompson was not one of the Tories' good old boys, being too formal in manner and too intelligent in approach to butter up the party hacks. Eventually he gained their respect, if not their admiration, but they lamented the fact that (unlike Sir John A.) there was an almost total absence of anecdotes about the man. The only quip recorded from his Ottawa days was that while dining at Government House one summer evening, when Lady Aberdeen suggested the windows be shut to keep out the unusually troublesome mosquitoes, Thompson replied, "Pray, don't trouble. I think they are all in now."

Abbott had got on by doing as little as possible – it was almost as if the prime minister's office had been empty those many months. Thompson would not get off so easily. The recession would continue to bite, and scandals that had been bubbling under since Macdonald's time would come to the surface during his tenure. But the source of his greatest problems would be a ghost.

Canada saw two prime ministers in 1892. John Abbott (left) governed from Macdonald's death until November of that year, when John Sparrow Thompson (right) took over.

That ghost was none other than the unquiet spirit of Louis Riel, the Métis mystic who led two rebellions, won provincial status for Manitoba and gained a sense of pride for his people. His miniature rebellions left most Canadians with a sense of disquiet – Canada has always been better dealing with functionaries than with rebels. Riel's quixotic mixture of statesmanship and fanaticism polarized the country for decades after his toy army was defeated at Batoche and he was tried for his life in Regina. During that 1885 court hearing, which marked a turning point in Canadian history, the Métis leader refused to hide behind a justified insanity plea that might have saved his life – and harmed his cause.

Louis Riel on trial in Regina, 1885. The question of Riel's fate divided Canada along religious and language lines and caused a deep rift in the Conservative party.

The hanging that followed swiftly created the young country's most enduring legend. A compelling and charismatic rebel in a nation of cloying and fastidious conformists, Riel posthumously fulfilled several sets of contradictory myths. Here was the brave French outcast who had sought only honour for his people, yet became the victim of Anglo-Saxon racial and religious prejudice. Here was the self-proclaimed holy man, a papist zealot who had murdered a loyal Orangeman (the unruly Red River prisoner, Thomas Scott) and deserved to die. Here, ultimately, was the prototypical Canadian hero – a well-meaning, self-deluded idealist who died prematurely by pretending to be sane.

The Parliamentary
Library in Ottawa
is all that remains of
the old Parliament
Buildings built in the
1860s. Before he was
offered the Liberal
leadership, Wilfrid
Laurier could be
found most days
curled up in a corner,
reading a book.

The emotional forces let loose by Riel's martyrdom were most harshly exploited by Honoré Mercier, leader of Quebec's militant Parti National, who turned the province's traditionally tranquil population into racially self-conscious mobs seeking vengeance. Perhaps because he realized that Orange Ontario was his bedrock political constituency, Macdonald showed none of his usual compassion in reviewing the many clemency requests for Riel's life. "He shall hang," declared the prime minister after refusing to commute the rebel's death sentence, "though every dog in Quebec should bark in his favour." Seventeen Tory backbenchers from Quebec walked out of the party. Dalton McCarthy, once a trusted Macdonald loyalist who had led a previous exodus of thirteen Tories to protest the prime minister's "pro-French" policy, began to cross the country, delivering vitriolic anti-Catholic speeches. Significantly, in the next federal election held after the execution of Riel, in 1887, the Liberals took Quebec for the first time since 1874.

The polarization of Canada along religious and ethnic lines was given a further boost in 1892 by a problem Thompson inherited from Abbott (who, of course, had done nothing about it): the Manitoba Schools Question.

In the aftermath of the Riel Rebellion, religious and ethnic intolerance continued to simmer along the banks of the Red River. In 1890 Manitoba was under the stewardship of a lacklustre Liberal named Thomas Greenway. In an attempt to save his faltering government by capitalizing on the anti-French feelings stirred up by visiting Ontario Orangemen, Greenway passed legislation abolishing French as an official language and withdrawing provincial aid from Manitoba's Catholic schools. In effect, that closed the separate school system, which had been guaranteed in perpetuity by the Manitoba Act that had created the province in 1870. The issue quickly grew into a national debate, pitting not only French against English and Protestants against Catholics, but involving the whole complicated issue of federal against provincial rights and church versus state.

Canada's supreme court unanimously invalidated the Manitoba law, which ought to have laid the issue to rest, but in July, 1892, the judicial committee of the Privy Council in Britain upheld the province's right to pass the legislation.

It had been the Tories' misfortune to latch on to one of those insoluble issues (like the Schleswig-Holstein question) that nineteenth-century politics seemed to glory in. Thompson asked the Supreme Court whether he could intervene. The court said no, but the matter went back to London for further study. In December 1894, Thompson died of a heart attack while visiting Windsor Castle, one month before the judicial committee decided that Ottawa did have the right to intervene. His successor, Mackenzie Bowell, an Ontario Orangeman who got the job because no one else wanted it, proved incapable of forcing the Manitoba government to restore French schools, and half his cabinet resigned. Finally, Bowell departed, and Tupper, Macdonald's aging "battering ram," took over on May 1, 1896. It didn't help, and the party went down to defeat on June 23, 1896.

He wouldn't have known it in 1892, but one man stood to benefit from this disaster. In 1891, Wilfrid Laurier had led the Liberals to defeat against Macdonald, in an unsuccessful attempt to end his party's thirteen-year stay in the wilderness. It must have been a humiliating experience. Laurier had not, originally, even wanted the Liberal leadership, only taking it on at the insistence of the former leader, Edward Blake.

Laurier has been eulogized in retrospect as Canada's saviour. "His supreme achievement was himself – a spirit of moral grandeur unique in the Canadian breed," wrote Bruce Hutchison in his book on Canadian prime ministers. "By the immeasurable dimensions of character none of our prime ministers could equal the serene, inward nobility of Laurier, his sunny spaciousness of soul, his delicate feminine touch, his mystical power over other men, his personal charisma. He was part saint, part autocrat, and part actor – a romantic in politics articulating his dream and Canada's." A generous assessment, but one that rings true.

For a man who did so much for Canada, it is worth noting that Laurier at first had opposed Confederation. After a brief period in the Quebec legislature, he became reconciled to the idea of a Quebec within Canada. He was elected to Parliament as a Liberal in 1874, beginning a career on the federal stage that would eventually span forty-five years.

Laurier served in the cabinet of Alexander Mackenzie and functioned as the chief of the party's Quebec wing. But after the Liberals were defeated in 1878 and 1882, he seemed to lose interest in politics. The newspapers nicknamed him "Lazy Laurier," and as the great John Dafoe of the *Winnipeg Free Press* would later recall, "The tall, courtly figure was a familiar sight in the Chamber and the library, particularly in the library, where he could be found every day ensconced in some congenial alcove."

No one knows what snapped Laurier out of his torpor and set him on the road to greatness. Perhaps it was actually being handed the Liberal leadership. Or perhaps, as Sandra Gwyn has suggested, it was the woman behind the man. The woman in question was not his wife, Zoë, but Emilie Lavergne, the wife of his old law partner. She and Laurier reputedly conducted an affair that lasted for decades, and there is even some speculation that he was the father of her son. Perhaps it was Emilie who shook him up and then saw him through the hard days after his defeat by Macdonald.

Whatever the cause, it worked. As the Conservatives grew more and more fractious, Laurier and his "sunny ways" of compromise grew more and more attractive. During the election of 1896 he was astute enough not to take sides in the Manitoba issue and instead depended on Quebecers to vote for one of their own. They did, and on June 23 Laurier was elected to lead the nation into the century that he confidently predicted would belong to Canada.

Wilfrid Laurier as he looked in 1891. The horseshoe pin in his cravat was a Laurier trademark, rather like the rose favoured by Pierre Trudeau.

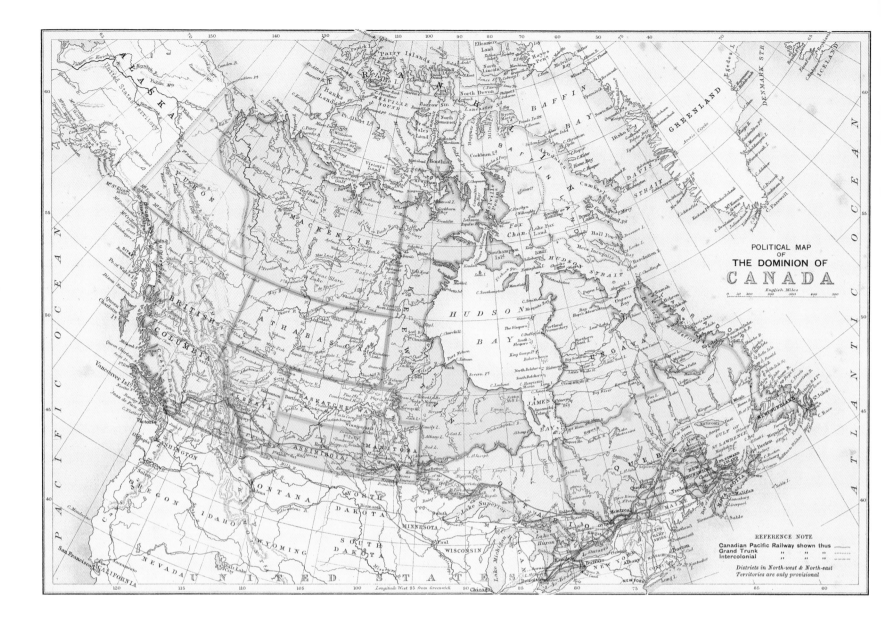

1892 : THE LOOK OF THE LAND

Glancing at an 1892 map of Canada is like looking at an old photograph of a familiar streetscape – the setting is the same but the details are different. In the map shown above, New Brunswick, Nova Scotia and Prince Edward Island appear as we know them today, but Newfoundland is a separate colony, having chosen not to join Canada at Confederation. Labrador, which was under Newfoundland's control, is just a narrow foothold on the edge of the continent. Where it ended, and Canada began, was uncertain.

Ontario and Quebec have their present-day southern borders, but what are now the northern areas of those two provinces were the territories of Keewatin and Ungava, part of the North-West Territories that had been purchased from the

Hudson's Bay Company by Canada in 1870. In the West, Manitoba had been carved out of those same territories in 1870, but much of what is now inside the province lies within the districts of Keewatin and Saskatchewan. The outlines of the future provinces of Alberta and Saskatchewan are visible in the districts of Alberta, Saskatchewan, Assiniboia and Athabasca. Paradoxically, Regina is not in the Saskatchewan territory but in Assiniboia.

British Columbia looks largely as it does today although there was some question as to where B.C. stopped and Alaska began. Although marked by boundaries here, the Yukon would not be separated from the North-West Territories until 1898.

Criss-crossing the map are thin red strands, marking the rail lines that played such a part in tying the country together.

A CHRONICLE OF THE YEAR

It was the year that brought the world Fig Newtons, *Vogue* magazine, cold cream, canned pineapple, book matches, *The Adventures of Sherlock Holmes* and Tchaikovsky's "Nutcracker Suite." Four hundred years after Columbus's first arrival in the New World, and two hundred and fifty years after Maisonneuve founded Ville Marie (later to become the city of Montreal), Canada was celebrating twenty-five years of Confederation. Life had never been better for citizens of the Dominion, who delighted in the marvels of public transportation, electric lights and central heating. Everyday tasks were made easier by such recent innovations as the telephone switchboard and the first truly sanitary bottle cap.

But while technology was progressing quickly, the pace of social change lagged behind. Clara Brett Martin's desire to become a lawyer was the force behind a private member's bill in the Ontario legislature which finally allowed women to study and practice law. But her 1892 victory was only partial; women were now permitted to be solicitors but were not allowed to plead in court as barristers. And other inequities abounded. Immigrants who did not fit the Anglo-Saxon mould found to their disappointment that almost every door in the promised land was closed to them. Children still laboured in factories, and the huge gap between the rich and the poor was only occasionally bridged by patronizing acts of charity.

Still, in its silver anniversary year, the infant Dominion had every reason to look forward to the next century. Settlement was expanding across the country and industrialization was raising the standard of living for all Canadians. Though ties to the Empire remained close, the sense of national identity so passionately asserted by Sir John A. Macdonald was growing stronger, giving Canadians the confidence to begin acting in their own national interest.

(Below) Harvest excursions, which took temporary labourers west to work on the harvest, helped fill the Prairies with settlers.

JANUARY

■ *January 9:* With a burgeoning population of seven hundred, Edmonton begins the year by incorporating itself as a town.

■ *January 16:* Pauline Johnson, hailed as Canada's "Mohawk Poetess," gives her first public reading at a literary evening sponsored by the Young Liberal Club of Toronto.

FEBRUARY

■ *February 2:* Canadians adopt the red ensign as their official flag. The flag consisted of a red field with a Union Jack in the top left corner and the coat of arms of Canada on the right.

■ *February 6:* The first instalment of a column entitled "At the Mermaid Inn" appears in the Toronto *Globe*. Each week poets Duncan Campbell Scott, Archibald Lampman and William Wilfred Campbell contributed short essays on subjects ranging from house-pets to philosophy.

■ *February 10:* Canadian representatives arrive in Washington, D.C., to discuss reciprocity (free trade). The delegations wrestled till the fifteenth, and emerged with no agreement.

■ *February 25:* The second session of the seventh Canadian Parliament opens under Prime Minister John Joseph Caldwell Abbott and meets until July 9.

■ *February 27:* What would become Pauline Johnson's most famous poem, "The Song My Paddle Sings," is published in *Saturday Night* magazine.

■ *February 29:* Legendary cowboy and ex-slave John Ware ties the knot with his sweetheart Mildred Lewis in Alberta.

MARCH

■ Governor General Lord Stanley announces this month that he will donate a silver cup, to be awarded at the end of the next year's hockey season, to the team with the highest standing. Future cup winners will be decided by a play-off.

APRIL

■ The North American Canal Company is contracted to deepen the St Lawrence River and build canals from Lake Erie to Lake Ontario in what will become one of the first phases of the Welland Canal system.

■ *April 14*: Windsor, Ontario, becomes a city.

■ *April 30*: St Anne's College at Church Point, Nova Scotia, is given university powers.

MAY

■ Sponsored by the Young Men's Hebrew Benevolent Society of Montreal and Baron Maurice de Hirsch, forty-seven Jewish families settle in Hirsch, North-West Territories (now Saskatchewan). Another group of persecuted Russian Jews who had arrived in the Territories earlier in 1892 received a chilly welcome from Regina residents. "Regina," they declared stoutly, "is not a suitable place to make a dumping ground for Russia's pauper element."

JUNE

■ *June 6*: Conservative members of Parliament commemorate the first anniversary of Sir John A. Macdonald's death by sporting a rose and a maple leaf – one to represent the old chieftain's favourite flower, the other his great patriotism.

■ *June 9*: Former Quebec premier Honoré Mercier is committed to stand trial at the October session of the Quebec Assizes for "conspiracy to defraud the Queen."

■ *June 14*: The first news is heard this year from the icebound coast of northern Labrador. Food shortages, gales and heavy ice had brought a winter of misery to the people on the coast and their situation was described as "extreme."

■ *June 30*: "The great curse of the Flowery Kingdom has raised its head in Toronto," shrieks the *Empire* as it breaks the sensational news that opium dens are operating in the city.

JULY

■ *July 1*: From coast to coast, Canadians celebrate the Dominion's twenty-fifth birthday with a free day of flag-waving, sports, picnics, speeches and fireworks. But in one ugly incident, an annexationist clergyman in Wiarton, Ontario, is forced by the town's leading citizens to take down the Stars and Stripes he had insisted on flying above the flag of the Dominion.

■ *July 8*: St John's, in the crown colony of Newfoundland, burns. The uncontrollable fire was started by careless smoking in a barn at a time when the main water supply was turned off for repairs. Before the fire was extinguished, 75 percent of the town had been destroyed and 11,000 people left homeless. English medical missionary William Grenfell arrived to see the smouldering remains of the once-prosperous town and immediately converted his ketch, *Albert*, into a floating hospital. This was the beginning of his career of good works on the east coast – by 1893 Grenfell had set up a working hospital at Battle Harbour and he lived to see his dream of a permanent mission, complete with schools and hospitals, come true.

■ *July 23*: Manitoba votes in favour of prohibition, although the legislation is never put into effect and business at the saloons continues exactly as before.

■ *July 30*: Britain's Imperial Privy Council upholds Manitoba's right to abolish separate schools in the province, setting off a national debate on language rights and federal versus provincial powers that continues to this day.

■ The summer of 1892 brings a typhoid epidemic to Regina, capital of the North-West Territories. Even though the city's first sewers had been installed the year before, sanitary conditions remained unspeakable and piles of waste could still be found at the end of every street.

AUGUST

■ Early this month the Mounties were called out in Calgary to prevent an angry white mob from attacking the town's Chinese residents. The near-riot began when a recent arrival, recovering from smallpox, was discovered in a Chinese-run laundry.

■ *August 9*: Seventeen-year-old aspiring author Lucy Maud Montgomery is thrilled when her grandparents give her permission to resume her studies at the local school.

■ *August 28*: The first meal in Canada to be cooked entirely with electricity is served at the Windsor Hotel in Montreal.

SEPTEMBER

■ *September 23*: Work begins in Perth, Ontario, on the world's biggest cheese. "Le Fromage Elephant," as the French papers called it, was made for display at the 1893 World's Exposition in Chicago. When finished, it measured twenty-eight feet around and weighed 26,000 pounds. As its fame grew, the mammoth cheese received visits from Governor General Lord Stanley, Minister of Agriculture John Carling, and other dignitaries. When it left Perth for Chicago on April 17, 1893, the cheese received a huge send-off from hundreds of townspeople and was serenaded by the local band. The monster triumphed at the exposition, winning 95 out of a possible 100 points.

OCTOBER

■ *October 3*: Painter Paul Peel dies in Paris.
■ This month Toronto's Osgoode Hall team defeated the Montreal Football Club to win the first Canadian Rugby Union Championship.

NOVEMBER

■ *November 3*: The first issue of the *Toronto Evening Star* appears on news-stands.
■ *November 4*: It takes only ten minutes for a jury to find former Quebec premier Honoré Mercier not guilty of defrauding the public treasury. His supporters carry him away from the courtroom in triumph, but Mercier's health is broken by his ordeal and he lives for only two years more.

■ *November 15*: Dr Thomas Neill Cream is hanged in London, England. His grisly career began in Canada, where he obtained his medical degree in 1876, but he left the country soon after, following a suspicious abortion case. Cream settled in the United States where he was jailed in 1880 for the murder of his lover's husband. Pardoned in 1891, he took his practice to England where on November 15, 1892, he was sent to the gallows for poisoning prostitutes with strychnine. His last words as he dropped to his death were reported as, "I'm Jack the...." The impact of this shocking near-confession was probably somewhat less than he had hoped – Cream was in an Illinois prison at the time of the Jack the Ripper crimes.

■ *November 24*: The Dominion's reluctant prime minister, John Joseph Caldwell Abbott, resigns. After only seventeen months in office, the man who had declared, "I hate politics" stepped down, complaining of ill health. The next day, John Sparrow David Thompson, who had been Macdonald's minister of justice (and, some believed, his more logical successor), was sworn in as prime minister. Thompson's major accomplishment in 1892 was the establishment of Canada's first Criminal Code. One of its articles – likely prompted by the falling birthrate among English-Canadians – made it an indictable offense to promote articles "intended or represented as a means of preventing conception or causing abortion."

DECEMBER

■ *December 15*: Canada's Amateur Hockey Association meets to plan its 1893 season, to begin on January 7, 1893. At the end of this season, the winner of the first Stanley Cup was the Montreal Amateur Athletic Association, which finished first over the Ottawa team.
■ The new home of the Ontario legislative assembly at Queen's Park was completed late this year and opened for the 1893 session on April 4, 1893.

THE LEGACY OF THE LAST SPIKE

"There will be no concluding ceremony, no nonsense," harrumphed Canadian Pacific Railway president William Van Horne as the completion of the transcontinental track drew near. But despite its lack of fanfare, the hammering-in of the CPR's last spike on November 21, 1885, remains one of Canada's most pivotal events.

Seven years later, the gleaming "ribbon of steel" that had fulfilled Confederation's promise of joining British Columbia with the East, was turning lumbering towns and buffalo bone dumps into burgeoning regional centres like Vancouver and Regina. (The CPR's Van Horne not only named Vancouver, he also sent out his surveyors after its devastating fire in 1886 to lay out and name streets. It was the CPR that decided the west end would house the wealthy, the east would accommodate the working class and the commercial district would sit in between.)

The "railway school" of Canadian art was born of another of Van Horne's schemes. The CPR gave Royal Canadian Academy members free passes to the West so they would paint the rugged Rockies and thus promote western rail travel. Tourism by train spurred the construction of those most distinctive of Canadian landmarks, the château-roofed railway hotels and 1892 saw work starting on the first of these CPR castles, the style-setting Château Frontenac in Quebec City.

In 1892 the railway also came to the British colony of Newfoundland. Conception Bay residents, aroused by tales of locomotives as destructive demons, battled surveyors, engineers and police for five days before being persuaded to accept their progress-driven fate. Not so fortunate in the battle with the demons of progress were the natives of the Canadian prairies. In 1882 Chief Poundmaker predicted that as soon as the transcontinental tracks were laid, "the whites will fill the country and dictate to us as they please. It is useless to dream that we can frighten them; that time has passed." Indeed, fifteen years later, Lady Aberdeen, the reform-minded wife of Canada's seventh governor general would lament that "these miserable specimens in dirty, squalid, coloured blankets haunt the railway stations." Soon those stations would become the disembarkation points for thousands of European immigrants, brought by rail to the prairie towns the railways had created.

(Previous page) A colour lithograph depicts Lord and Lady Stanley admiring the view from the cowcatcher when crossing the Rockies by train in 1889. (Right) Westbound trains started their runs from the platforms of Montreal's Windsor Station, the nerve centre of the CPR. (Far right) The completion of the CPR in 1886 by no means marked the end of railway building in Canada. These workmen are celebrating the completion of the Calgary & Edmonton Railway in 1891, just one of the many lines that were snaking their way across the empty land. (Bottom) Keeping the railway running required almost as much effort as building it. To service the trains, railyards, workshops and buildings like this handsome roundhouse at North Bay were being built all across the country.

(Far left) By 1892, Canadian Pacific was not only transporting people across the country, it could also take them to the very ends of the earth thanks to its fleet of ocean liners. (Top left) For those with more humble tastes, day or holiday excursions were becoming popular. (Bottom left) As this poster suggests, the country was truly united from one coast to the other by 1892. (Opposite) CPR President William Van Horne, an art collector and amateur painter, sent Canadian painters west at the railway's expense to record their impressions. Painter Lucius O'Brien captured this train passing through the Rockies on a trip he made under CPR sponsorship in 1886.

SEAPORTS AND CITADELS

The Atlantic Region

HALIFAX
THE LAST IMPERIAL GARRISON

BY 1892, FAR FROM BEING THE dominant economic force it had been during the bonanza days of the wind ships, Halifax had settled into a comfortable niche as a commercial seaport and the last of Canada's garrison towns.

The nineties marked the beginning of the end of a way of colonial life, but while it lasted, nearly everyone seemed to enjoy the experience. The garrison's young officers devoted most of their energies to skimming about the harbour in sloops out of the Royal Nova Scotia Yacht Squadron, or to galloping their mounts over the lawns of Fort Needham for some energetic chukkers of polo. They continued to gamble on the illegal cockfights held at a pub on St Margaret's Bay Road, but no longer defended their honour by challenging one another to duels.

With the Age of Sail drawing to a close and the increasingly centripetal pull of the National Policy favouring industries located in Ontario and Quebec, the Halifax economy by 1892 had been seriously weakened. Fortunately, help was at hand. In the mid-1880s, the British government had decided to reinforce what it grandly called its "marine quadrilateral" – the bases at Malta, Gibraltar, Bermuda and Halifax. Technical advances in warship design, the increased power of explosives and the introduction of breech-loading guns had made these ports' older fortifications obsolete. Throughout the 1890s, Halifax's elaborate defensive installations were extensively reconstructed, even if no one seemed sure who the harbour guns were supposed to be aimed at, or why. Still, that vague call to distant action helped invigorate the sleepy garrison town.

With their commercial battles behind them, Halifax's powerful and inward-looking local Establishment now spent their days intermarrying and clipping coupons. The mansions of the upper crust, built mainly in the city's south end (between Tower Road, South, Inglis and Barrington streets) were their private playgrounds, when they weren't wintering in Bermuda or at their summer places in Chester, but the Royal Navy base (which wasn't fully turned over to Canada until 1910) was the centre of society life.

From the beginning Halifax had been intended as a garrison town, but the city's superb year-round harbour and its location as the first mainland port on the route from Europe to North America also made it the natural choice as the hub of East Coast trading. In the early nineteenth century, the most prosperous of Halifax's venture capitalists were engaged in a triangular trade – fish in return for tropical products from the West Indies, which were shipped to Britain and the Continent.

Halifax's geographical advantages spawned an active shipping community led by Samuel Cunard who in 1839 founded the first trans-Atlantic ferry service, which would eventually take passengers across the Atlantic in five days. But, by mid-century, the city had also seen the establishment of such major financial institutions as the Halifax Banking Company, the Bank of Nova Scotia, the Union Bank of Halifax and the Merchants Bank of Halifax, which later became the Royal Bank of Canada. Halifax even had an early stock exchange, trading periods being limited to three sessions a week, starting "at ten minutes after the firing of the noon gun from the Citadel." After 1876, when the Intercolonial Railway was completed to the East Coast (joining the Grand Trunk at Rivière-du-Loup), local cotton mills, shoe factories and sugar refineries began to flourish, though the Nova Scotia capital remained more of an administrative and financial centre.

The social season ran from June to November, when the Royal Navy admiral was in residence (he wisely spent the winter months at his Bermuda station), and local hostesses vied for invitations to one of his "at homes." The chosen few were invited aboard the admiral's flagship for Sunday service and the elaborate buffet that followed. "Sometimes social life is pleasantly mixed with local charities," reported a contemporary gossip columnist. "Last year anybody who was any body, and many who were nobody, joined hands and had

a grand bazaar for the benefit of 'The Sailors' Home.' The ladies were all in sailors' dress. There was everything to attract the eye, tickle the palate, and empty the pockets of the thousands who flocked to the Exhibition Building where the bazaar was held."

Although Halifax was a navy town, a British line regiment was also stationed there and the Grand Ball at its Wellington Barracks was the annual society highlight, with elaborate ploys practised to keep chaperones occupied while their charges danced the night away.

Basking in an imperial glory that would itself soon fade, Halifax took a bow as Canada's last Royal Navy garrison town – and started a slow retreat from centre stage.

Halifax harbour from Citadel Hill.

(Right) A tennis party given by Lady Clanwilliam (centre) at Admiralty House in 1886. On the far right in mutton-chop whiskers and gold braid is Admiral Clanwilliam, the commander of the Royal Navy squadron stationed at Halifax. In the summer months when the fleet was in, Admiralty House served as Halifax's naval and social headquarters. Today, Admiralty House (above) is home to the Maritime Command Museum.

Halifax's Jubilee Bandstand
(below) was erected in the city's
Public Gardens in 1887 to
mark the fiftieth year of Queen
Victoria's reign. With a band
playing on a summer afternoon
(left), it evokes life during the
golden afternoon of Empire,
right down to the nearby
allegorical statue of Flora,
goddess of flowers.

61

British soldiers were stationed at Halifax's citadel, presumably to protect the naval base from invasion. (Right) Peacetime soldiering in the Queen's army had its perks, as these polo-playing officers on Citadel Hill could attest. (Below) The army garrison on church parade.

For off-duty sailors (left), the preferred place of relaxation was Upper Water Street, which was lined with saloons and hotels. In some ways, Halifax had more in common with Portsmouth or other English naval towns than it did with inland Canadian cities.

Among the many improvements the Royal Navy made at Halifax was constructing a graving dock (left) in 1889, which made it easier to make repairs on ships' hulls. (Above) A coast guard ice-breaker enters the dock, still in use a century later.

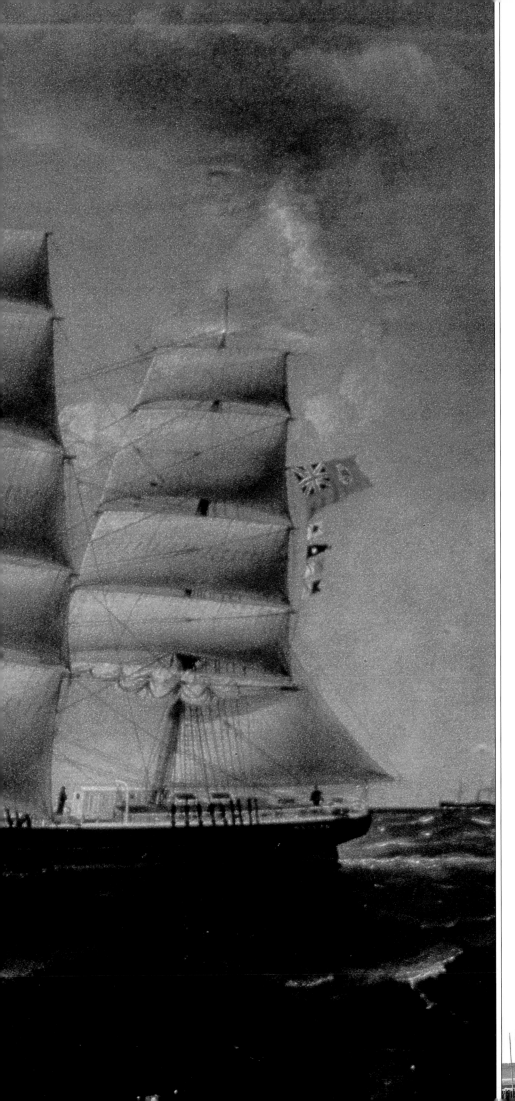

B y 1892 Canada's brief, bright age of sail had passed. Waterfront communities sighed for the return of Canada's stature as one of the greatest shipbuilding nations in the world, when the tidal terminal of nearly every creek and river was marked by the angular silhouettes of the great wind ships.

While it flourished, construction of these salty thoroughbreds set new maritime standards. More than 4,000 ships, each exceeding 500 tons, slipped down the launching ways. Obedient to the call of the offshore breezes, Canadians sailed their ships on every trading route. By 1878 some 7,196 merchant ships, aggregating 1,333,015 tons, were registered at Canadian ports, giving the sparsely settled new Dominion the world's fourth-highest sea-going tonnage. These illustrious wind ships – so graceful that even when heavily loaded they scudded before the softest breeze – carried grain, timber, coal, whisky, ice, whale oil and other products to ports on four continents.

Canada's abundant growths of virgin timber at water's edge had been directly responsible for the birth and success of shipbuilding. While English and European yards fashioned their ships of oak and teak, Canadian vessels, known as softwood ships, were mostly constructed from hackmatack (also called larch or tamarack), pine and spruce. The seaworthiness and low cost of the Canadian wind-jammers were a revelation to the British and Continental builders. *(Continued)*

(Left) The full-rigged Bluenoser
Ruby *under sail. (Below)*
Spencers Island, Nova Scotia,
was a centre of shipbuilding
on the East Coast. Here, the
Glooscap, *one of the last*
of the square-riggers, nears
completion in 1891.

67

At first, these ships were sold on world markets, but after 1840 most were operated by Canadians, particularly in the South American, West Indian and African trades. Yarmouth, Nova Scotia, for example, owned more tonnage per capita than any other port in the world. It entered 2,000 vessels on its registry – most of them built in the district. Local shipowners grew so wealthy they formed their own insurance companies and two banks – the Bank of Yarmouth and the Exchange Bank of Yarmouth.

By 1892 more and more of the world's better-paying cargoes were being carried by steel tramp steamers. Low freight rates and high insurance premiums had made the operation of sailing vessels uneconomical. The construction of Canadian square-riggers declined rapidly and ceased completely by 1895, although the building of three-masted schooners continued for some years. Shipowners sold their wind ships for little more than salvage values.

The switch from wood to steel did more than the change from sail to steam in ending the prosperity of Canadian shipbuilding. The yards might have survived if Canada's steel mills had been better developed. A few of the more efficiently operated sailing ships tried to buck the coming of the steamboats, but theirs was a lost cause, and Canada's great fleet of wind ships gradually vanished from the world's oceans.

For true Maritimers, the sea was a family affair. Edmund Spicer (right) was one of four brothers who spent their lives under sail. His brother George commanded the Glooscap, *shown on the previous page, and Edmund's ship the* George T. Hay *(far right), photographed here at New York, was also built at Spencers Island, where the family had lived since the American Revolution.*

ATLANTIC SEAPORTS

St John, New Brunswick (right), was in decline by 1892, although its fortunes improved after 1895 when it became the winter port for eastern Canada. Yarmouth, Nova Scotia (far right), could boast that more ships were registered there than in any other Canadian port. (Below) Living by the sea shaped the social habits of Maritimers, giving rise to such customs as this chowder party on the beach at Pease's Island, Nova Scotia.

"A VERY HAPPY YEAR FOR ME"

"I feel happier and more contented today than I have felt for a long time," seventeen-year-old Lucy Maud Montgomery recorded in her diary on August 9, 1892. "It was decided to-day that I am to go to school here again."

"Here," was of course Prince Edward Island, a place that she would one day fix in the imaginations of readers around the world. After spending a year with her father and stepmother in Prince Albert, Saskatchewan, the future author of *Anne of Green Gables* had returned to her grandparents' farm in Park Corner, P.E.I. There, Maud, as she was known, spent her days teaching a little music and writing poetry. But she desperately wanted to go to Charlottetown's Prince of Wales College to study for a teacher's licence. And like her red-haired heroine, she had had to fight for what she wanted: "Grandpa and Grandma have always been so bitterly against it that I was getting discouraged."

Her Anne-like determination must have prevailed however, for by mid-August she was back at the local school preparing for the college entrance exams. As 1892 rolled to an end she wrote, "I am sorry to see it go for it has been a very happy year for me."

A goal for L.M. Montgomery (top) in 1892 was to attend teachers' college in Charlottetown.

(Below) Prince Edward Island's capital as it appeared in the early nineties.

THE OLDEST COLONY

Although Newfoundland had been invited to the first conferences regarding Confederation, the colony had decided not to join Canada in 1867. Twenty-five years later, Newfoundland still went its own way, eking a difficult living from the sea. Life on the Rock was difficult at even the best of times, and for the citizens of the capital, St John's, 1892 was a disaster. On July 8, a devastating fire swept through the city, consuming hundreds of wooden buildings, and ultimately doing some twenty million dollars' worth of damage.

Wilfred Thomason Grenfell took Newfoundland by storm when a catastrophic fire was doing the same to its capital. Aboard the *Albert*, a ketch ship that also functioned as a floating church and hospital, Grenfell entered St John's harbour in July 1892 to the stench of smouldering ash. His timing couldn't have been better – or his mission more pressing.

Grenfell embraced a "muscular Christianity" that stressed action rather than doctrine. Leaving an 1885 revival meeting in England with fire in his belly, the twenty-year-old medical student resolved "either to make religion a real effort to do as I thought Christ would do in my place as a doctor, or frankly abandon it." Seven years later, after learning of the abject poverty along North America's easternmost shores, the British Deep Sea Mission to Fishermen grudgingly sent the inexperienced Grenfell on an exploratory tour of Newfoundland and Labrador.

After his timely arrival in St John's, Grenfell's task was clear. Working free of charge, he supplied the city's two physicians, clothed some of the fire's hardest hit and opened up the *Albert* to the sick and curious. By contrast, the Church of England bishop, notes Grenfell biographer Ronald Rompkey, "launched an appeal to rebuild his stone cathedral while the faithful went unclothed, unhoused and unfed."

Grenfell then left for Labrador where he encountered everything from lung disease and scurvy to beriberi, rickets and arthritis. Because the colonial government provided only one medical officer, doomed to hop from port to port on a few hours of sleep every night, people were skeptical when Grenfell arrived, often asking, "Be ye a real doctor?" Three months after coming to the "land of dog, cod and fog," as he affectionately dubbed it, Grenfell had treated over 900 people.

Envisaging a permanent mission that would dispense medicine, education and the gospel, Grenfell returned to Britain and embarked on the first of his legendary fund-raising tours. Years later Grenfell's "great northern parish" would be served by schools, hospitals, co-operative stores and a medical mission whose work, based in St Anthony, Newfoundland, earned him a knighthood and a place alongside Livingstone in the pantheon of larger-than-life Victorian heroes of the Empire.

(Below) The young Wilfred Grenfell (centre) with a group of Moravian missionaries during his visit to Labrador in 1892.

73

HEIRS OF NEW FRANCE
Quebec

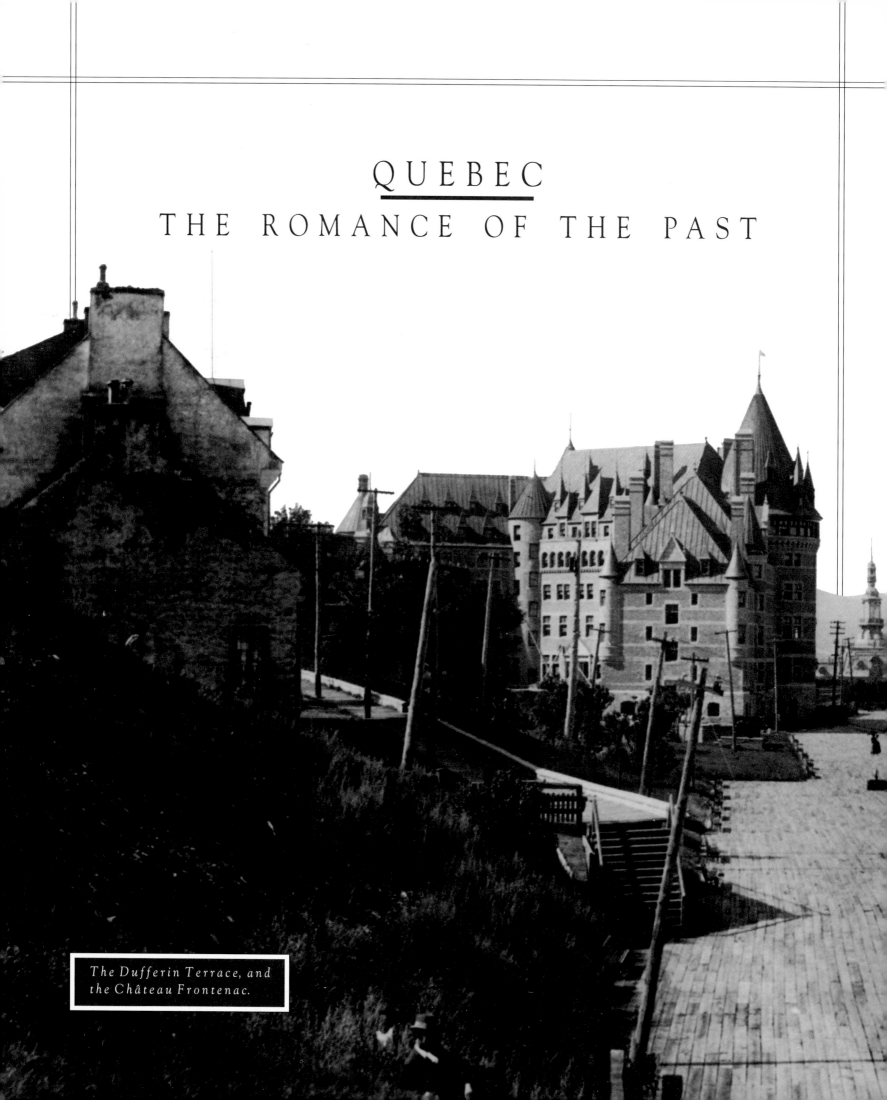

QUEBEC

THE ROMANCE OF THE PAST

The Dufferin Terrace, and
the Château Frontenac.

THE NAPOLEONIC WARS THAT shook Europe between 1793 and 1815 had been the economic making of Quebec. Britain, cut off from its regular Baltic timber supplies, had turned to Canada as an alternative, especially for the magnificent tall trees that could be fashioned into masts for the men-of-war that formed the Empire's first line of defence. Most of the timber trade came through Quebec City, the only major port on the St Lawrence River that was then accessible to ocean-going sailing vessels. Founded in 1608, the walled city had also served as the administrative centre for New France and, later, British North America.

The decline of the timber trade (which peaked in 1810, with 661 ships being cleared out of Quebec City) coincided with the introduction of trans-Atlantic steamships and by the 1890s Quebec's magnificent harbour, watched over by the squat fortifications of the Citadel, had become a bit of a backwater. That trend was reinforced by the 1865 transfer of the federal government to Ottawa.

But the real reason for Quebec City's loss of importance was, of course, the rapid rise of Montreal. The dredging of a channel up the St Lawrence enabled ocean-going vessels to sail on to Montreal and consolidated the larger city's dominance of overseas trade. As well, Montreal's expanding role as the terminus of the new railways crossing the Dominion meant that the city became Canada's commercial capital. Quebec's prospects were further hurt by the fact that it was totally bypassed by the boom in railroad building. The only railway that approached the region was the Grand Trunk, which in 1854 extended its line to Lévis on the opposite bank of the St Lawrence. It took another quarter of a century before the first steam engine pulled into Quebec City, and a local bridge across the river wasn't opened until 1917.

But Quebec remained the provincial capital, and as such was a powerful player in the always-tense game of federal-provincial relations. And the city was discovering a new role. Its fortified walls, steep cliffs and narrow streets – its "Old World" charm – were proving an increasingly powerful tourist draw in the late eighties and nineties, a time when the romance of the past was gripping the public imagination. Chief among the city's fans had been Lord Dufferin, who, as governor general, had taken to spending part of the year in residence at the Citadel. He encouraged the city fathers to preserve the old cliffside walks, the most famous of which, the Dufferin Terrace, today bears his name.

By 1892 the draw of Quebec was strong enough to warrant the opening of the Château Frontenac, a hotel overlooking the St Lawrence River. Designed by the American architect Bruce Price for the staunchly imperial Canadian Pacific Railway, the Frontenac, in keeping with its romantic location, was designed in a mock-French fashion that became known as the "Château" Style. This style spread, until the centre of virtually every large Canadian city was dominated by an outsized French château put up by Canada's competing railways to house their customers.

Designed by Eugène-Étienne Taché, and completed in 1885, Quebec's Drill Hall (below) shows a strong French influence in its turrets and spires, a fore-runner to the Château Style that would become so popular a few years later. (Right) Big guns outside the armoury, 1891.

(Far left) Details from the Drill Hall's ceiling. (Left) This monument, erected near the hall in 1891, commemorates the deaths of Short and Wallick, two British soldiers who died fighting one of the numerous fires that swept Quebec City in the nineteenth century.

"French" architecture in Quebec came to the fore with Philadelphia architect Bruce Price's Château Frontenac. Shown (left) not long after it was completed, the hotel facade bears the names of the French explorers who figure prominently in Quebec's history. (Below) Much extended and enlarged, the Château still dominates Quebec City's cliffs.

Completed in 1884, Quebec's National Assembly (left) was also designed by Taché. (Below) The Green Chamber (recently painted blue for television) is where the National Assembly meets. (Opposite) Formerly the home of Quebec's upper house, the Red Chamber is now used for cabinet meetings.

(Far left) Honoré Mercie[r]
encouraged Quebecers to
establish farms in isolated
parts of the province, such
as this one near Lac-St-Je[an].
(Left) Berthier-en-haut
(today Berthierville) was [a]
typical Quebec town on
the St Lawrence.
(Right) A barge on the
Chambly Canal, near the
English town of St Johns
(now St-Jean-sur-Richelie[u]).

THE QUEBEC DIASPORA

Nineteenth-century rural Quebec is commonly viewed as a living Krieghoff painting where happy habitants tilled their ancestral farms by the St Lawrence, beneath the twin spires of the local church and the *curé*'s watchful eye. But even one hundred years ago, Quebec was a society in the process of transition.

Factory jobs, especially in New England, were pulling people from the land. Some of those leaving were farmers giving up on marginal land, others were farm workers who had lost their traditional work with the widespread shift to dairy farming. But whatever the cause, more than half a million, mostly rural, Quebecers left the province after 1870, to work the mills of towns like Lowell, Massachusetts. By 1900 they made up an astonishing ten percent of New England's population, a French-Canadian diaspora, now almost wholly assimilated, its only legacy the many French names still found today in New England.

For nationalists like Honoré Mercier, who saw their nation, and their influence, literally packing up and moving away, and Quebec's ultramontane churchmen, who worried about losing their flocks to a secular, urban life, steps were needed to reverse the tide. Under the government's Ministry of Agriculture and Colonization, directed by the popular Curé Antoine Labelle, new areas of the province, such as Temiscamingue and Lac St-Jean, were opened up. In some cases families of twelve or more were offered one hundred acres free, but few chose the hardship of homesteading on what was often marginal farmland as long as other, better paying jobs were available.

As the 1890s wore on, the population drain away from rural Quebec continued, but with a change. Those leaving were more and more often heading for Montreal or Quebec and new jobs in those cities' growing industries. French Canada would not vanish into New England's mills, but the change from a docile rural population to an increasingly urban one would have profound long-term effects on life in the province.

(Left) This barn, at Cap à l'Aigle, combined old-World thatch with New-World squared logs in a distinctly Quebecois structure. Cap à l'Aigle was near Murray Bay (now La Malbaie) a popular resort town on the St Lawrence.

THE FATHER OF QUEBEC NATIONALISM

For fiery Quebec nationalist Honoré Mercier, 1892 was the year of the fight of his life. Already stripped of office, financially ruined and with his party defeated, Mercier had been charged in April of that year with accepting bribes and thus faced the very real threat of jail. For a politician who had so recently been the champion of French-Canadian nationalism, the spring of '92 was the winter of his discontent.

The son of a man who had fought with Papineau in the rebellion of 1837, the Jesuit-educated Mercier had been raised from earliest childhood with a deep belief in France, Quebec and the church. An early opponent of Confederation, he only accepted it after Quebec's Catholic bishops announced their support. Trained as a lawyer before he moved into journalism, Mercier had spent some time in federal politics, but it was on the provincial scene that he excelled. Elected provincially in 1879, he became premier in January 1887, after his Parti National was swept into power on the crest of emotion unleashed by the hanging of Riel two years earlier.

During his five-year tenure as premier, Mercier broke new political ground. Perhaps as a way of repaying his old teachers, Mercier brought in the Jesuit's Estate Act, which compensated the order for lands lost after the British conquest of 1759. Negotiating this act was a delicate process that saw Mercier dealing directly with church figures in Quebec, Pope Leo XIII, and various nervous Protestant groups. In what was a first, he appointed a Catholic priest, Curé Antoine Labelle, as a deputy minister in his government, in the new provincial Ministry of Agriculture and Colonization. This department was created to encourage the settlement of isolated parts of Quebec and to stop the flow of French-Canadians heading for the opportunities of New England. Mercier also called Canada's first premiers' conference to champion provincial rights – a conference to which Ottawa was pointedly not invited.

Mercier's life-style matched his ambitions for Quebec. He resided in a magnificent residence on Quebec City's Rue St Pierre and owned a large seigneury at Sainte-Anne-de-la-Perade, where he set up a luxurious stud farm. As premier he travelled throughout Europe, calling on the Pope,

gathering foreign decorations, and acting, to the consternation of many English-speaking Canadians, more like a head of state than a provincial premier.

Mercier's problems began in 1891 not long after his return from Europe. Ernest Pacaud, the Liberal treasurer, was accused of accepting $100,000 from the syndicate chosen by Mercier to complete the Baie des Chaleurs railway, and some of that money, it was alleged, had ultimately found its way into Mercier's pockets.

The popular premier's career went into a rapid decline. Following a royal commission

(Above) Honoré Mercier (seated second from left) called Canada's first conference of provincial premiers on October 26, 1887. (Inset) Curé Antoine Labelle, a deputy minister of Mercier's, was the first Catholic priest to hold a government office in North America.

Mercier in bronze (above) is the only statue that stands today on the grounds of Quebec's National Assembly. (Below) A period cartoon of the premier.

investigation into the scandal, A.R. Angers, the province's lieutenant governor, dismissed Mercier as premier in December 1891. His party lost the election five months later, although Mercier managed to hold on to his seat. In April 1892, Mercier and Pacaud were called before the Quebec Assizes, charged with accepting bribes and held for trial. In June he declared bankruptcy. Finally, in October, ten months after he had been removed from office, Mercier was put on trial – and found not guilty. Spectators who had followed the case agreed that Mercier had aged remarkably during his ordeal. But although he would continue to be plagued by ill health, he stayed on in politics for another two years, serving as leader of the opposition. Mercier never lost his nationalist outlook, and in a speech he gave in April of 1893, one widely regarded as his political swan-song, he laid out his philosophy for the people of Quebec: "Men, women and children, it is for you to choose; you can remain slaves under colonial status, or become independent and free, among other people who invite you to the banquet of nations."

THE COMMANDING CITY

Montreal

MONTREAL
THE NEW-WORLD LAIRDS

IN 1892 MONTREAL WAS THE Capital of Victorian Canada, both in terms of its animating entrepreneurial spirit and imperious financial clout. Confident in its tranquil possession of power, the city's commercial aristocracy controlled not only the province of Quebec but two-thirds of Canada's wealth and most of the major corporate institutions in the country at large. The robber barons who conducted the nation's business were ruthless in the exercise of their authority, and yet there was about them a sense of the urbane, a faith in manners and a deep respect for privacy and the proper order of things.

Montreal's excellent natural harbour had been the spur for its original growth. Later, Canada's two great national railways, the Grand Trunk and the Canadian Pacific, were headquartered in the city to collect raw materials for export and distribute foreign goods. By the early 1890s, however, Montreal had become more than a transportation terminus. Several industries had grown into significant employers: sugar-refining, flour milling, wood processing, shoemaking, textile milling, tobacco-product processing, and railway rolling-stock manufacturing among them. With a population of more than 250,000, Montreal also had the advantage of a large pool of skilled labour. But the well-springs of corporate power remained the Canadian Pacific and the Bank of Montreal, with no one ever quite certain which of the two institutions controlled the other.

While a true aristocracy was supposed to be based in generations of ownership and cultivation of land, Montreal's rich and powerful were much newer arrivals – mostly the same men who had built the railways, dug the mines and financed the mills. They were called "Square Milers" because most of their mansions were located within an area roughly a square mile in size, bounded by McGill University on the east, Dorchester Street to the south, Guy Street on the west and Pine Avenue on the north on the lower ridges of Mount Royal. As they harvested their fortunes and turned to spending their money as ostentatiously as possible (a task made easier by the fact that Ottawa, at this early date, collected no income tax), the Square Mile's rather ordinary streets were transformed into a pageant of baronial castles, Florentine palaces and Tuscan villas – *arriviste* architecture writ large. The interiors of the Square Mile houses were so opulent

Montreal Harbour from the customs house.

that tables practically buckled under the weight of Oriental vases, brass Indian serving trays and other ostentations. A bare spot on a study wall or an under-decorated drawing-room corner was thought to signify a lack of wealth, and there was always an elephant foot, buffalo head, stuffed owl, ostrich egg, or ceremonial Japanese sword to fill the void. "The overall effect was pompous," noted June Callwood in a history of the period, "but not without a certain innocent, unselfconscious charm."

Such grand settings required royalty and nobility – knights, lords, kings and queens – and if the real thing wasn't available, their colonial cousins would have to do. That meant entertaining Canada's governor general and his chatelaine so incessantly that the vice-regal couple virtually became honorary Square Milers, attending the inauguration of nearly every toboggan slide, cricket challenge and cultural soirée. It also meant that the Square Milers themselves competed fiercely for British titles, with half a dozen peerages and two dozen knighthoods eventually granted to the Canadian aspirants.

The work ethic and pleasure principles of these nabobs were so widely shared that they seemed less arbitrary attitudes than God-given commandments. Their world was tidy. Identities were secure and every emotion was set in its proper context. Modes of behaviour were either prescribed or forbidden. A man was judged by how he disposed of the pits when eating cherry pie. And even though the model for all this forbearance and rectitude might have seemed English, in fact it was not. The giveaway to the real source of all these moral codes and uptight attitudes was the manteltree kettle that dangled over most of the mansions' fireplaces – a replica of the traditional cooking implement that had been so much a part of the Scottish hearth.

Though they worshipped all things English and could barely contain themselves whenever they glimpsed a member of the Royal Family, most of the Square Milers marched to the drummers who had sounded the muffled roll-calls at Culloden. The Square Mile was never little England. It was a Scottish diaspora, and it was the kinship rooted in the rock-hard allegiance to their clans into which these men had been born that formed Canada's first business Establishment.

Their ethnic solidarity and shared values, their bonding and networking, allowed them quickly to become dominant in forging the economic links of the new Canada. They bought land when it was cheap (or preferably got it for free) and industrialized a landscape that had barely been changed since the arrival of the first Europeans. They succeeded where their predecessors had failed because they were shrewd yet apprehensive, stubborn yet resourceful, capable of creatively combining commercial avarice with public purpose. Irish navvies and Chinese labourers built the CPR, but the Scots ended up owning it. Among the merchants who formed the Bank of Montreal in 1817, five were Scots. James Muir, later the head of the Royal Bank, always had his St Andrew's Society speeches published in private editions, their covers bound in his tartan.

Foremost among these New World lairds was Lord Strathcona. Strathcona (who had been born plain Donald Alexander Smith and spent the first three decades of his professional life as an ordinary HBC fur trader in Labrador) became such a snob that he actually kept a private guest tally, categorizing his visitors according to their social rank. His impressive roll-call – which accurately reflected the glitter of the Square Mile's 1892 social life – included a future king and queen of England, a prince and princess, 8 dukes, 7 marquises, 21 earls, 6 viscounts, 6 governors general, 7 prime ministers, 27 provincial premiers, 4 archbishops, 17 bishops, 14 chief justices, 29 supreme court judges, 31 mayors, and 58 generals. (Ever the stickler for the subtle distinction, Strathcona further separated his generals according to whether they were British army or colonial troop commanders.)

Befitting his social position, Strathcona boasted one of the greatest of the Montreal mansions, which spread across two properties at Fort and Dorchester streets. Its exterior was brownstone

and the massive front door opened opened onto a magnificent three-storey, $50,000 mahogany staircase, carved by artisans who had dovetailed all the parts so that there was not a single nail in its construction. The second-floor ballroom was overlooked by a marble balcony large enough to accommodate a small orchestra. The dining-room opened into a garden that could hold more than two thousand visitors. Below stairs and out of hearing was a row of eight rooms for a butler, a dozen maids and assorted flunkies.

Even more ostentatious was the mansion built by Lord Mount Stephen, the Scottish carpenter's son who along with his cousin Strathcona had been the main fiscal agent in the CPR's construction. His palatial quarters at 1440 Drummond Street (now the Mount Stephen Club) were built in the Italian Renaissance style, surrounded by an English garden that covered most of a city block. The house, which took three years to build, featured an entrance hall carved entirely out of Cuban mahogany, doorknobs and hinges plated with twenty-two-carat gold, and panels of

St James Street, the city's financial heart.

seventeenth-century stained glass. The walls of its master bedroom were carved in bird's-eye maple and no door in the house was less than four inches thick.

Although upper-class Montreal was a very British place, the city itself had become increasingly French since mid-century. Not that this switch had bothered Montreal's Square Milers much. As Lord Strathcona explained in one of his speeches, "Though we have in Canada a portion of the population who had not originally come from Great Britain, I can say without hesitation that they are just as good and loyal British subjects as ourselves. They are Englishmen with only one difference – that they speak French as well as English!" So much for bilingualism 1892-style.

In vivid if less noticed contrast was yet another Montreal, usually referred to as "the city below the hill," where the working classes lived a very different kind of existence. The worst of these districts was Griffintown, a poor Irish ghetto, where the streets were either unpaved or covered with a mixture of cobblestones and tamarack blocks and children sometimes walked barefoot the year round. The houses, often tar-paper shacks, were only a few minutes' walk from the Square Mile, but in terms of lifestyles they might as well have been on another planet. Montreal, then as now, was not just one city but a metropolis of several communities, each spinning in its own orbit.

(Right) Market day in Jacques Cartier Square. The business life of Victorian Montreal was dominated by the English presence, but this open-air market, with Montreal's city hall in the background, attests to the city's French-Canadian character. The column, however, is a memorial to Lord Nelson and is similar to those found in other capitals of the Empire. (Above) The square and the city hall today. Gutted by a fire in the 1920s that left only the walls standing, the city hall was rebuilt with a roof that is two storeys higher, and crowned by a cupola in place of the old tower.

(Right) Place d'Armes in 1892. The imposing building on the left is the New York Insurance office which, when completed in 1888, was Montreal's first skyscraper. In contrast to this monument to Anglo Mammon is Notre Dame Church, at right, sometimes referred to as the parish church of French Canada. (Below) The New York Insurance building today. (Opposite) Painter Robert Harris's depiction of a leafy Montreal square gives an impression of how Place d'Armes must have looked in summer a century ago.

(Right) Sherbrooke Street was the main avenue of Montreal's Square Mile where the city's business élite built their mansions. But some of the rich (above and below) were moving out along Dorchester Street to Westmount, which remains Montreal's choicest neighbourhood.

CONTRARY COUSINS

They were rich, related and unrelenting rivals. Both were born and raised in Scotland and had come to Canada as young men. But Donald Smith, shown above, did not meet his cousin, George Stephen, seen right, until 1866 when he was forty-six and Stephen thirty-seven. Their first meeting did not go well. On a visit to Montreal, Smith, who was serving a long-term posting in Labrador as a Hudson's Bay Company factor, decided to look up the cousin he had been told was a prosperous man in the woollen trade. George Stephen, already a

citified success, was apparently not impressed by the backwoods style of his bushy-bearded relative.

But the two men stayed in touch. Smith used the nest-egg he had amassed in Labrador to invest in Bank of Montreal shares. In what was to become a pattern, Stephen followed Smith's lead and by 1873 had become a director and leading share-holder of the bank. During the years that followed, – with Smith rising to the top of the Hudson's Bay Company, Stephen to the presidency of the Bank of Montreal and the CPR – Smith's keen business sense led his cousin into increasingly lucrative ventures. As David Cruise and Alison Griffiths put it in Lords of the Line, "Smith was the instigator and catalyst and Stephen the consummate deal maker and financier...Smith's rare sense of where to find

the money...led Stephen into his most profitable investments: the Bank of Montreal, the St Paul and Pacific Railroad and the CPR."

Although Stephen became the Canadian Pacific Railway's first president, it was Smith who held the hammer and was the central figure in the last spike ceremony in 1885. Stephen had higher honours in view, being made a baronet that same year and advancing to the peerage in 1891 with the title of Baron Mount Stephen. Although Smith's collaboration had contributed enormously to his wealth and elevation, Stephen rarely showed appreciation or even consideration towards his cousin. When he resigned from the presidency of the CPR in 1889, he announced his decision at a director's meeting with no prior warning to Smith. When Smith protested this treatment, Stephen told him he was being a "baby."

In 1892 Stephen took a lease on Brocket Hall in Hertfordshire and settled in to enjoying life as an English lord. Smith followed him to England in 1896 as High Commissioner to London and the following year he too joined the gilded circle as Baron Strathcona and Mount Royal. By the turn of the century Stephen and Strathcona could number themselves among the world's wealthiest men. But even after Strathcona's death in 1914, Stephen could not bring himself to speak well of his rival. To a writer working on a biography of Strathcona he refused assistance and wrote that his cousin's contribution to the building of the railway that united Canada was "ancient history and of little or no consequence to anyone."

102

THE RAILWAY MAGNATE'S MANSION

Today many of the grand old mansions that once lined the streets of Montreal's Square Mile are gone or greatly altered. Fortunately, one still remains in something like its original condition. George Stephen's house (left) is now the exclusive Mount Stephen Club. Although the old conservatory (above) is gone, the main staircase (opposite) gives an impression of how the house looked a century ago (top and far left). By 1892 Stephen was living in England, and his sister and her husband, the industrialist Robert Meighen, were in residence.

Montreal in 1892 was the capital of Canadian medicine. McGill University had the country's foremost medical school and, on the lower slopes of Mount Royal, the new Royal Victoria Hospital (made possible by donations from Montreal's two most prominent philanthropists, Donald Smith and George Stephen) was nearing completion. A rather forbidding building to modern eyes, the Royal Victoria in 1892 represented the last word in hospital design.

Montreal's pre-eminent position in medicine was largely the doing of one man, Dr William Osler. Hired as a professor by McGill in the 1870s, he pioneered the notion that becoming a doctor required not just lectures, but actual hands-on experience of anatomy, and the use of such advanced teaching aids as

(Below) Dr William Osler revolutionized medical studies throughout North America.

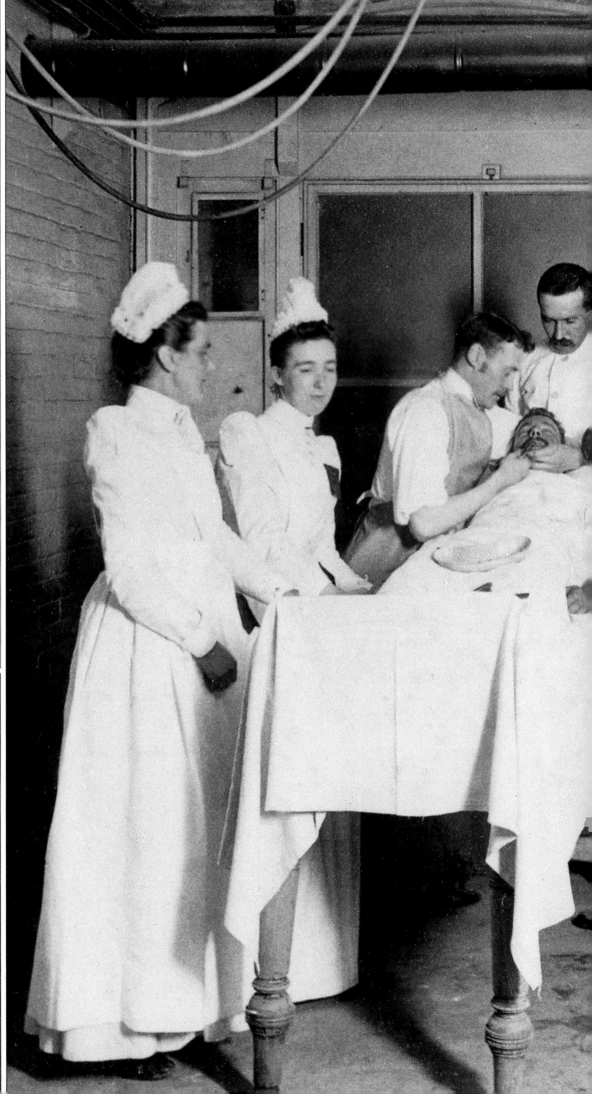

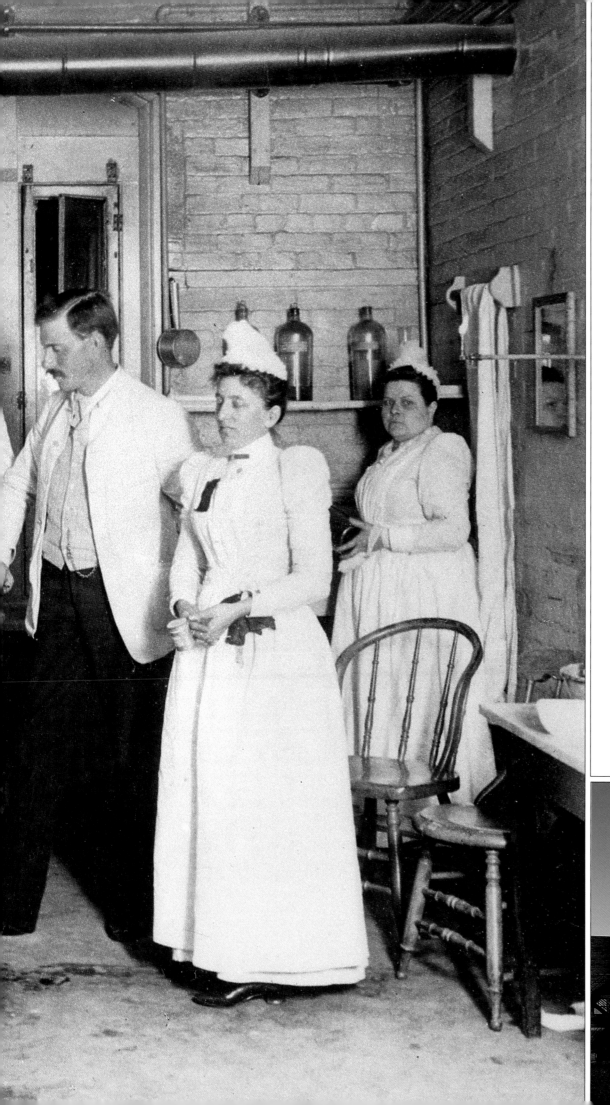

microscopes. By 1892 Osler had left McGill, but the school still followed his methods. And, thanks to the publication that year of his *The Principles and Practice of Medicine*, those ideas were spreading throughout the world.

Despite the advances of Osler and other medical pioneers, medical practice in the late Victorian era was still relatively primitive. Surgery was limited largely to amputating gangrenous limbs, although hygienic procedures were becoming more prevalent as was the use of ether and chloroform as anaesthetics. Many Canadians, especially in rural parts, stuck to older folk cures, treating asthma with a quick walk around the house at midnight or strep throat by pressing a yellow toad to the afflicted area. Patent medicines were an enormous business in the late nineteenth century and their manufacturers made extraordinary claims for their products, which were frequently useless concoctions of herbs laced with alcohol. Nonetheless, Dr Williams' Pink Pills for Pale People were said to work wonders and St Jacobs Oil was guaranteed to conquer pain.

(Left) Neither a mask nor a pair of gloves is in sight in this operating room at Montreal General in 1892, and dust is clearly visible on the overhead pipe. (Below) Royal Victoria Hospital today.

105

THE ROMANCE
OF WINTER

Perhaps because they couldn't escape it, Canadians a century ago celebrated winter. (Left) Every year Montreal held a winter fair, the centre-piece of which was an imaginative, multi-storey ice castle. (Below) On Saturdays the Tandem Club put their sprightly two-horse sleighs through their paces on the slopes of Mount Royal. (Bottom) Another fixture of Montreal winters were the toboggan slides in Mount Royal Park, here recreated indoors at William Notman's studio.

THE RISE OF SPECTATOR SPORTS

In the early 1890s, sports in Canada were well on their way to becoming the big business they are today. For the more privileged, joining a tennis, golf or snow-shoeing club served a social purpose as well as a recreational one. But a real sign of change was in the crowds going to the ball parks or the new indoor hockey arenas, not to play, but to watch.

The two biggest spectator sports of the 1890s were hockey and baseball. Toronto and Hamilton both had teams in the International Baseball League, and eventually eighteen professional clubs played in Canada. Hockey was growing in popularity too, although truly professional hockey was still at least a decade away. Everyone seemed to be interested in it, even the governor general's two sons, who took to the ice for the vice-regal home team, the Rideau Hall Rebels. And, although they couldn't have known it, next year when the Montreal Amateur Athletic Association team took to the ice in January at the start of the 1893 season, a Canadian tradition was born – they would, when the season was over, become the first winners of the Stanley Cup.

Tennis (below) and other racket sports enjoyed increased popularity in the 1890s.

(Right) The trophy room in the Montreal Racket Club's headquarters, built in 1889.

(Left) The first winners of the Stanley Cup, the Montreal Amateur Athletic Association, pose with the trophy that Lord Stanley had donated in March 1892 to honour Canada's top amateur hockey team. Whether it was cricket (near right), baseball (middle right) or hockey (far right), most athletes played just for fun.

A POLITICAL COCKPIT
Ottawa

OTTAWA
THE NATION IN MINIATURE

N A VISIT TO OTTAWA IN 1872, Goldwin Smith dismissed the town as a "sub-arctic lumber village transformed by royal mandate into a political cockpit." A cruel dismissal, but like so much of what Smith said, it was not altogether inaccurate. By 1892 Ottawa had progressed, but still there were complaints. "To me," wrote one local, "Ottawa has ever been Ottawa. That is taxes and desolation."

At the centre of Ottawa life in the 1890s was the governor general and his toy court at Rideau Hall. Being named governor general of Canada was a real plum, often a stepping stone to becoming viceroy of India. But in the case of the 1892 incumbent, Lord Stanley of Preston, it was really a pre-retirement reward for years of faithful, if uninspired service to Her Majesty. Stanley had been a close confidant of Sir John A. Macdonald, although he had preferred to exercise his influence behind the scenes. During his tenure, Government House began to entertain industrialists and VIPs from across the country, turning the official vice-regal residence into what historians Bernard Ostry and H.S. Ferns called "a social hierarchy, gilded and plumed…such as no other city in North America could display."

Away from Rideau Hall or the great Gothic mass of the Parliament Buildings, the political centre of Ottawa was the Russell House hotel, at the corner of Sparks and Elgin streets. Originally a relatively modest stone structure, the Russell House had expanded along with the government, until by the nineties it was a four-storey Victorian pile, taking up the better part of a block. For many MPs, or "sessionals" as they were somewhat derisively

tagged by the city's permanent residents, the Russell House was home while the House was sitting. Sit in the lobby, the word was, and all the world would pass by. But the real action was in the Hotel Bar, which stood off the lobby. It was there that the deals were cut, the lobbyists pressed their cases, and the votes of members and senators were bought and sold.

Befitting its status as the nation's capital and home to more than 37,000 people, Ottawa in 1892 had many of the amenities associated with big city life. Electric lighting had been introduced in 1885 and six years later, the first streetcars appeared in the city's central core. New buildings, appropriate to Ottawa's size and importance, were also being constructed. In 1889, the Langevin Block, across from the Houses of Parliament was opened. Planned as the home for much of the then-embryonic civil service, the four-storey block was designed in a Gothic style that echoed the Parliament Buildings, and named for Hector Langevin, the minister of works. Ironically, Langevin was forced out of office in 1891, after it became public that money for projects under his ministry's direction had been funneled into his own political war chest. Another building of the time, the Central Chambers, built in 1890, was designed as offices for the growing numbers of lawyers and other professionals who were making the city their home.

Despite these changes, Ottawa in 1892 was not really one big town, but many smaller ones. Lower Town, the oldest part of the city, was a collection of grey stone buildings, constructed in a simple, classical style that showed a certain French influence appropriate to the neighbourhood of the city's Francophone population. Buildings in Upper Town and Sandy Hill, home to the civil servants and to the city's growing professional class (mostly English-speaking Protestants) were usually constructed of Victorian brick. Upper Town's Sparks Street looked like the main street of a small Ontario town. Le Breton Flats, where many of the Irish lived, was a collection of small workers' cottages, built for the labourers in the lumber mills.

Comfortably ensconced in cliffside mansions overlooking the river, the lumber barons still controlled the city economically. Their vast log rafts covered the river and their mills, built near the Chaudière Falls, lined its banks. By the 1890s, the government dominated local society, but the better-behaved or more respectable of the lumber barons were welcomed into it. E.B. Eddy, the owner of the largest match works in the British Empire, was regarded as a little eccentric, but his company was more acceptable than that of John Rudolphus Booth. No matter that Booth's mills were, by 1890,

the largest producers of sawn lumber in the world, there were standards, and his foul language and love of chewing tobacco tended to exclude him from polite company.

The lumber business peaked in 1896 and then, aided by a disastrous fire in 1900, which destroyed many of the mills and left thousands homeless, slowly declined. Good wood was disappearing from the Ottawa Valley, and most of the remaining lumber barons were too old and too set in their ways to respond to new challenges. The disappearance of the timber business left Ottawa a one-industry town. But in 1892, Ottawa – part-French and part-English, Catholic and Protestant, with self-made lumber tycoons on the one hand and mill workers on the other, watched over by the sovereign's representative and her public servants – was a fairly accurate microcosm of the country it governed.

Timber slide near the Chaudière Falls.

(Above) The Parliament Buildings have changed, and so has the city around them, but the river and the steep cliffs lining it have not. Seeing them today, one can easily recognize the same scene from one hundred years ago (left).

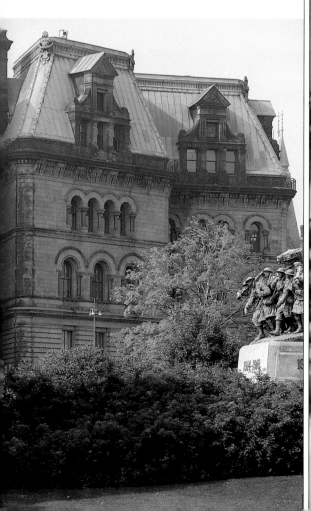

(Right) Ottawa's Elgin Street in the early 1890s. When completed in 1889, the Langevin Block, visible here on the right, and as it looks today (below), was big enough to house virtually every federal civil servant. The fence that separates Parliament Hill from the street (above) provides another recognizable link with the city's past.

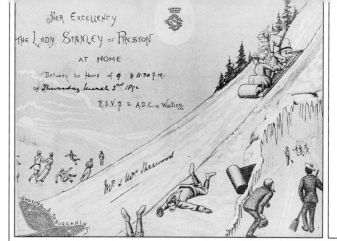

THE STANLEYS: JUDGEMENT AND TACT

Every day unwitting tributes are paid to one of Canada's least memorable governors general. Whenever Canadians refer to North America's most coveted hockey prize, they evoke the name of Lord Stanley, sixth governor general, who donated the cup named after him to the Dominion and then complained about the fifty-dollar cost of the original bowl.

Frederick Arthur Stanley, sixteenth Earl of Derby and Baron of Preston, was born in London in 1841. After holding numerous cabinet posts, including secretary of state for the colonies, he readily accepted the offer to represent Queen Victoria in Canada.

The Stanleys arrived in Montreal in 1888 with four of their ten children. When Lady Stanley set foot in Rideau Hall, the official residence that Queen Victoria insisted be called "Government House" as in every other colonial capital, she cringed at the "hideous blues and reds." Upon vacating the residence in 1893, she warned her successor about the "very old-fashioned" furniture. Moreover, "the walls are absolutely bare.... The room which has always been the wife of the G.G.'s sitting room is very empty.... There are no lamps in the house at all. No cushions, no table-cloths, in fact none of the small things that make a room pretty and comfortable."

But the limitations of Rideau Hall did not cramp the Stanleys' style for grand entertainments. Although they liked to be in bed by midnight, the vice-regal couple hosted all the galas expected of the closest thing to Canadian royalty. Their albums contain mementoes of skating parties, dress up carnivals, sleigh rides, a cakewalk in the middle of Lent and theatricals starring family members. R.H. Hubbard recorded that "for one splendid party" at Quebec City's Citadel, where the Stanleys spent their summers, "the rooms were hung with bunting and cooled by blocks of ice; on the terrace, decked with green boughs and Chinese lanterns, were little tents for spooning."

Yet Lady Stanley was anything but a superficial socialite or an amateur "at-homer." Judged by Liberal leader Wilfrid Laurier to be an "able and witty woman," she founded a since-demolished nurses' training institute on Ottawa's Rideau Street.

The G.G. himself never seemed happier than when he was "killing salmon" at Baie des Chaleurs, Quebec. Such an avid angler was he that, as Sandra Gwyn notes, he "built for himself a cosy nineteen-bedroom fishing lodge, which he named Stanley House, and installed in it one of the first rural telephones in Canada, for the express purpose of calling to points upstream to find out how the salmon were rising."

In political life Lord Stanley was influential, but quiet about it. Despite the burying of three prime ministers, the inauguration of two others and the eruption of many more nation-threatening issues, his tenure is everywhere described as "unexciting." This is not to say that Stanley withdrew from Canada – traversing the country by train, horseback and boat and surveying the diverse scenery (of which Vancouver's Stanley Park is a fitting example) invigorated him. It was this youthful energy guided by decorum that won people's hearts. "In Canada," read a standard tribute after his departure, "Stanley won much popularity; he encouraged imperial sentiment in the Dominion, and... had full scope for the exercise of his judgement and tact."

Lord Stanley (above) and Lady Stanley (left). (Far left) Dressed as cheerful habitants, Lord Stanley and his entourage are ready for a day of snow-shoeing at Rideau Hall, 1889.

POETS OF THE CIVIL SERVICE

"His mind is erratic and slovenly, but there is some good stuff in it, which comes out now and then…," wrote the young Ottawa poet and civil servant Archibald Lampman to a friend in February of 1892. The object of Lampman's backhanded praise was his next-door neighbour, fellow poet and civil service toiler, William Wilfred Campbell. Campbell, Lampman continued, was an "odd fish" and "deplorably poor" from working in a temporary government clerkship for $1.50 a day. To help him out, Lampman and his friend Duncan Campbell Scott (also a fledgling writer and civil servant) had approached the Toronto *Globe* "to give us space for a couple of paragraphs and short articles weekly at whatever pay we could get from them." Thus was born "At the Mermaid Inn," a weekly collection of short essays, reviews and observations that ran for less than a year and a half but, for what it reveals of literary life a century ago, occupies a significant niche in the history of Canadian writing.

The first column appeared on Saturday, February 6, 1892, and contained a contemplative piece by Lampman about the Canadian seasons as well as a brief aside on Kaiser Wilhelm II's surprising fondness for Mark Twain. Scott contributed a review of Victor Hugo's last poem and Campbell a paragraph about the class system in North America. For three dollars each per week, the young writers continued to send in their eclectic *pensées* for the Saturday column – on pets and sea serpents, Trappist monks and open fireplaces, alongside more serious examinations of literary and political developments in Canada and abroad.

As if to reinforce Lampman's earlier assessment of him, Campbell's "good stuff" appeared less regularly than that of the other two. And shortly after he landed a better-paying position with the Department of Militia and Defence in June of 1893, the column ended altogether. In one of his final contributions Campbell presented some nasty poem parodies by one "John Pensive Bangs" for whom Lampman was the obvious model.

Lampman's reputation withstood this satire, and, despite a career cut short in 1899 by his death at the age of thirty-eight, he is today regarded as the finest of Canada's late Victorian poets. Duncan Campbell Scott lived until 1947 and championed Lampman's poetry throughout his life while carving out his own reputation as a major Canadian poet. William Campbell became an ardent exponent of

(Above, centre) Ottawa's Central Post Office as it looked when Lampman (right) worked for the Postal Department.

British imperial greatness and died in 1918. In 1976 the *Globe and Mail* revived for a time "The Mermaid Inn" with an opening column by Hugh MacLennan.

STANDING ON GUARD

The stone-battlemented armouries that are familiar landmarks in many Canadian towns are a legacy of the time when Canada's best hope of defence lay in its militia. With only a tiny standing army, the Dominion relied on its part-time soldiers to protect its nascent borders from threats, external and internal.

But in 1892 the Canadian militia wallowed in trouble. Smart, well-disciplined and patriotic on the surface, its grubby soldiers and gentlemanly officers lived an existence very much in need of dramatic reform.

Once a year soldiers and officers suffered together for a fortnight at summer camp where, fortified by inadequate rations, they engaged in repetitious drills and the occasional sham battle for the benefit of tax-paying spectators. For the other fifty weeks the few permanent corps privates pocketed less than half the wage of common labourers, slept in cramped quarters and could not even look forward to pensions. Officers were no better off, earning less than half of what their American counterparts did and receiving no allowance upon retiring.

In fact, crass patronage fuelled Victorian Canada's defences. Given that so many officers sat in Parliament, it's no

wonder militiamen wielded clout – and corrupted the force. "The greatest difficulty I found," admitted Major-General Ivor Herbert during his reform blitz of the early 1890s, "was in checking abuses which…have been tolerated by the government for the benefit of their political supporters. Men were brought to camp who were quite unfit for service, and put on the pay lists though it was never intended that they should do a day's drill. Officers absented themselves without leave, and their places were taken by others without any authority and frequently persons holding no commissions at all were entered on pay lists as officers…."

Why did so many men put up with low morale and even lower pay to serve in the Canadian militia? For starters, money – any amount during an era of serious economic hardship – came in handy. For the more privileged who could dream of officer status (their dreams belying its reality), the militia opened doors to approval, even admiration. Above all, duty meant a break from the grind of work and family. It offered lasting friendships and fond memories, typically improved by booze. In between sham battles and weekly parades, the Canadian militia of the early 1890s was ripe for reform.

(Below) Whatever its shortcomings as a military force, the Canadian militia could not be bested when it came to uniforms. This period poster shows the elegant rig favoured by various regiments of the Canadian militia.

RED-BRICK VICTORIANS
Toronto and Ontario

TORONTO

FORTUNES ON THE RISE

I N THE 1890s, TORONTO WAS still a harbour city. Wharves filled with warehouses and offices stabbed out into Lake Ontario, turning the shoreline near Bay and Yonge streets into Toronto's busiest commercial district. Freighters bearing Lehigh Valley coal (worth $1 million annually) landed regularly at the foot of Church Street. Arrivals and departures of the passenger vessels sailing to and from other Great Lakes cities or on pleasure excursions to Niagara or up the St Lawrence were great social occasions, while the ships themselves boasted salons equipped with marble-topped tables, overstuffed sofas and stained-glass windows.

A busy metropolis of 185,000, Toronto had become the greatest beneficiary of Sir John A. Macdonald's National Policy, as attested to by the growing number of industrial smoke-stacks on the city's skyline. But Toronto's boosters had long realized that no matter how favourable the industrial climate might become, they could never compete with Montreal unless their city became an important railway terminal. They set about accomplishing precisely that. The first set of tracks, completed in 1853, connected the city with Barrie to the north, and two years later an extension was built as far as Collingwood on Georgian Bay. At the same time, Toronto was connected into the Great Western Railway system, which gave its merchants access to Windsor, Detroit and Buffalo. A link with Montreal through the Grand Trunk, and the fact that canal ships could move Toronto's goods down the Erie Canal to various U.S. ports on the sea, transformed the city into an important export centre.

Electrification of Toronto's factories triggered a boom in heavy industry, with 2,500 major manufacturing enterprises busy turning out consumer products by 1892. Such activity required heavy financing and Toronto's banks – among them the Commerce, Toronto, Dominion, Standard and Imperial – kept pace with the force-fed industrial growth, as did the new loan and mortgage houses, such as Canada Permanent Mortgage and Freehold Loan & Trust. Among the most influential bankers of the period was Robert Henry Bethune, who spent twenty-four years as general manager of the Dominion Bank. According to the historian

Donald Creighton, "Bethune seems to have been almost a caricature of the faceless banker. There appears to be no record of anything he said or wrote." Indeed, Bethune was so retiring that he didn't even speak at the bank's annual meetings. But however colourless, he knew banking. One of his innovations was to change the way money was lent. Instead of relying on promissory notes signed and often guaranteed by prominent citizens, he taught his staff to assess a borrower's individual worth and the value of his or her collateral.

A very different character was Sir Henry Pellatt. Pellatt got his start working in his father's stock brokerage at a time when such investment dealers (others prominent at the time were E.B. Osler and A.E. Ames) were on the rise. Pellatt's Toronto Electric Light Company obtained the franchise to light Toronto's streets. He was also involved in the hydroelectric development at Niagara Falls and later joined the syndicate that formed the Toronto Railway Company, the private investment group that introduced streetcars to the city. An eccentric millionaire (who once had a set of false teeth made for his horse) Pellatt later built Casa Loma, his grandiose ninety-eight-room castle that featured mahogany stalls for his horses and was once described as being "half 19th century Gothic and half 20th Century Fox."

Outside Montreal, Toronto was the only Canadian city that could afford to maintain the trappings of social class in all their Victorian intricacy. At the time the *nouveau riche* were families like the Eatons and the Masseys, whose fortunes, it was said, "needed time for mellowing." Shopkeepers (the Eatons) and manufacturers (the Masseys, who had moved their operations to Toronto from Newcastle about fifty miles east of the city in 1879) were deemed to be only marginally acceptable, compared

Looking south from Queen's Park, 1892.

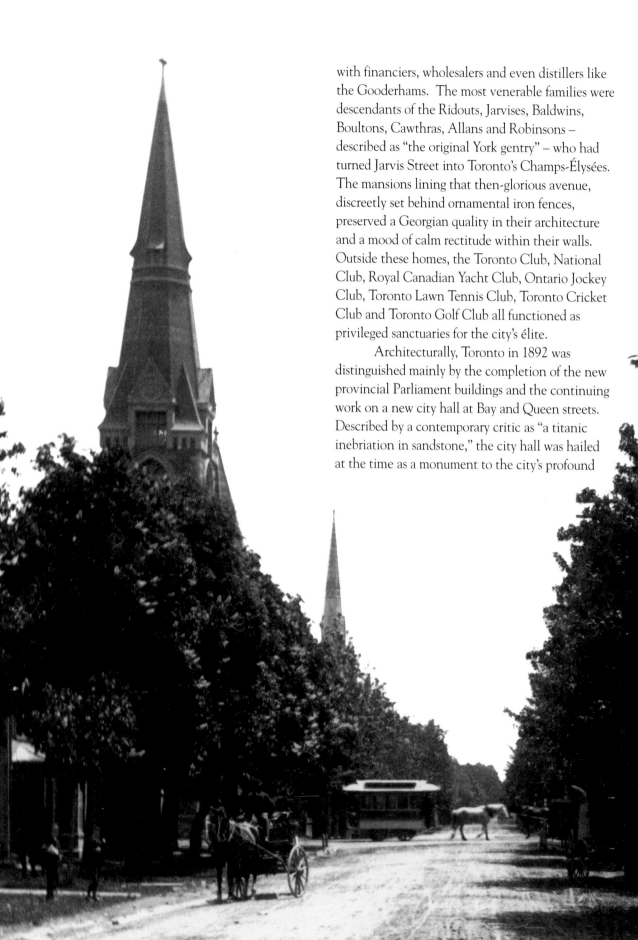

with financiers, wholesalers and even distillers like the Gooderhams. The most venerable families were descendants of the Ridouts, Jarvises, Baldwins, Boultons, Cawthras, Allans and Robinsons – described as "the original York gentry" – who had turned Jarvis Street into Toronto's Champs-Élysées. The mansions lining that then-glorious avenue, discreetly set behind ornamental iron fences, preserved a Georgian quality in their architecture and a mood of calm rectitude within their walls. Outside these homes, the Toronto Club, National Club, Royal Canadian Yacht Club, Ontario Jockey Club, Toronto Lawn Tennis Club, Toronto Cricket Club and Toronto Golf Club all functioned as privileged sanctuaries for the city's élite.

Architecturally, Toronto in 1892 was distinguished mainly by the completion of the new provincial Parliament buildings and the continuing work on a new city hall at Bay and Queen streets. Described by a contemporary critic as "a titanic inebriation in sandstone," the city hall was hailed at the time as a monument to the city's profound ultra-Victorianism – elegant but serious. When the Romanesque pile was finally finished in 1899, at twice the original cost, the building was launched with a rare bit of showmanship. On that grand and glorious day Toronto's aldermen were driven to its massive front door in two streetcars drawn by twelve white horses. There, to the thump of a massed military band, one of them unlocked the building with a gold key made by Birks.

Jarvis Street, from just above Carlton.

Most of the city's architectural imagination went into building Toronto's churches. It was the most over-churched city in North America. "There are churches on every corner," complained the social critic Arthur Peach. "On the other corners are schools. There seems to be plenty of religion with very little Christianity." Toronto was overwhelmingly Protestant, and Protestant in a very dour way, which meant one could do nothing on Sundays except go to church (although some Methodists sanctioned the occasional Sabbath picnic). Theology was the order of the day, with each denomination fiercely arguing for its own tenets and attacking those of its less holy rivals. To be an Anglican gave you an edge, socially, over the Presbyterians, and God alone looked after the Methodists. Religious beliefs became most serious when Orange Protestants clashed with Irish Catholics – an all too frequent event.

Christianity was not yet much concerned with social issues, let alone social action, and the poor of the era, when government assistance was meagre at best, had to depend on the frigid and patronizing charity of the rich. According to the ethic dominant at the time, men and women were poor because they drank too much or were possessed by some fatal flaw in character. Many of Toronto's moneyed classes felt the best solution to poverty was to crusade against the sale and manufacturer of liquor. (Being the most religious place in Canada didn't prevent Toronto from consuming more rye whisky than any place on earth; anyone who drank less than twenty ounces per sitting was regarded as a teetotaler.) The more enlightened sponsored havens, homes and missions for "the wayward and the helpless."

By 1892 Toronto was a large city; it had yet to become a great one. Its economic and social classes had been evolving in isolated enclaves, hardly aware of one another's existence. It would take the maturing process of another few decades before Toronto would come into its own – and begin overtaking Montreal.

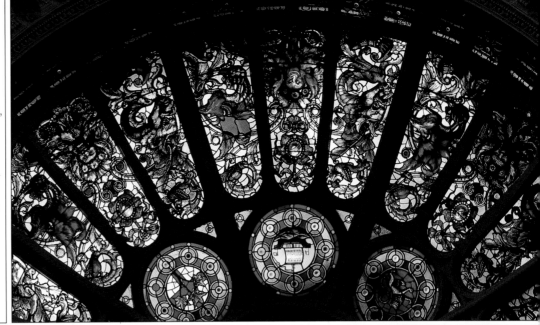

(Below) A view of Yonge Street, looking north from Front in 1892. The building on the left was the office of the Bank of Montreal, completed in the mid-eighties during a period when rival banks were vying to put up the most impressive structure in the city's thriving commercial centre. The bank's interior featured a two-storey high banking hall, still capped by a stained-glass dome (right).

THE RAGE FOR ROMANESQUE

(Opposite) Richardsonian Romanesque, the style named for H.H. Richardson, the Chicago architect who developed it, enjoyed great popularity in the early nineties, perhaps nowhere more than in Toronto. The exterior details shown here are from two of the city's finest Romanesque buildings, the Ontario Legislature and the Gooderham Mansion (now the York Club), both completed in 1892. The stained-glass window is from Toronto's old city hall, another Romanesque building then under construction. (Left) The Gooderham Building, also completed in 1892, for distiller George Gooderham (owner of the Gooderham Mansion), was in a slightly more subdued style known as French Gothic.

LIGHTS OF A CITY STREET

(Left) Completed in 1894, Frederic Marlett Bell-Smith's Lights of a City Street is an accurate depiction of the intersection of Yonge and King streets, as the slightly earlier photograph (below) shows. Bell-Smith also had fun with his painting. The policeman on the sidewalk is Bill Redford, the constable who, normally, really was on duty at this corner; Bell-Smith himself is shown to his right, buying a paper; and the artist's son is the moustached man raising his hat.

BUILDING QUEEN'S PARK

Upon their completion in 1892, the imposing Romanesque buildings that still house Ontario's legislature in Queen's Park were more than just a place to conduct the business of government, they were an emblem of Ontario's new prosperity and its pride.

Plans for a new legislature had begun back in April 1880 with the announcement of an international competition. More than a dozen designs were submitted, but with a budget limit of $500,000, even the winning entry was deemed too expensive to build. The project was shelved until 1885 when the budget was raised to $750,00 and R.A. Waite, an English architect living in Buffalo, was called in to decide between the winning design and the runner-up. Declaring neither design suitable, Waite announced, as the *Canadian Architect and Builder* of 1890 explained, that "he was the only architect on the continent capable of carrying out such important work."

By 1890, construction costs for Waite's design had risen to over $1 million, and the price-tag of the building was used, unsuccessfully, as an election issue against Premier Oliver Mowat's Liberals. But when Ontario's new legislative buildings were finally completed, probably even the staunchest Tory felt some pride. Except perhaps the Conservative member F.W. Marter, who had promised a hat to every lady in two rural townships if the new building came in at "one cent less than $2 million." According to the Toronto *Evening News*, Marter owed 842 lucky women new hats.

(Left) Although Queen's Park suffered a serious fire in 1909, the east wing was undamaged and today looks as it did when completed in 1892. (Right) This rather formidable statue of Queen Victoria sits in front of the legislature. (Below) The centre block under construction in the early nineties.

SUMMERTIME

Finding a summer retreat by the water was already a Canadian custom a century ago. For the rich, that could mean a castle in the Thousand Islands (far left), while for humbler folk, camping out (left) on Toronto's islands had to suffice. (Below) Frederick Challener captured the essence of those long-ago summers in his A Song at Twilight, *painted in 1893.*

F. S. CHALLENER 1893

THE PROTESTANT CAPITAL

T oronto in the 1890s was the most Protestant city in the world, a sort of Calvinist Tehran, watched over by the black-suited mullahs of the local Protestant denominations whose followers made up eighty percent of the city's population.

Although the varying Protestant denominations were said to have their differences – Anglicans were rich, Presbyterians shrewd, and Methodists poor but pious – there was one issue that fired every Christian heart. With the exception of some suspiciously Romish high Anglicans, all the churches dearly wanted to preserve the glittering jewel in the crown of Toronto rectitude, the Lord's Day.

To say that there was nothing to do in Toronto on a Sunday in 1892 was an understatement. The theatres were closed, and sports, even rowdy games, forbidden. In fact, the city started to wind down the night before, with saloons closing by seven, presumably to give imbibers plenty of time to sober up before service the next morning. And in January 1892, the keepers of Toronto's Sunday had won a great victory: in a citywide plebiscite, the citizens of Toronto the Good had defeated a motion by the city's horse car line to run cars on Sunday.

The Sunday car supporters had pointed out the benefits to the humble working man of being able to use the cars on his day off, perhaps to travel into the country where, in the midst of nature's sublime beauty, his lungs filled with fresh air, he could recharge himself. The opposing forces, nicknamed the "Saints," argued that Sunday cars were the thin edge of the wedge. "First, Sunday Cars," said the Reverend T.A. Rodwell of Agnes Street Methodist Church, "second, Sunday newspapers" and then, suggested the preacher, even greater outrages, leading finally, and perhaps most frighteningly, to "the organ grinder and the peanut vendor on the street corner."

Faced with such terrifying prospects, the city's voters had taken the only course open to them as good Protestants – good *Toronto* Protestants – they refused the evil pleasure of taking Sunday rides on horse cars.

Although Methodists were typically seen as simple, pious folk, like the family depicted at prayer in George Reid's painting (below), Toronto's Metropolitan Methodist Church (left), often referred to as that denomination's "cathedral," had a well-heeled congregation, which included Hart Massey.

(Right) Whatever their views on strict Sabbath observance, Toronto's Protestants were not immune to sensory delights, and some of their churches had beautiful interiors. St Paul's Methodist (later converted to St Paul's United and now to offices) featured art-nouveau angels painted by Toronto artist Gustav Hahn in the early nineties.

SCHOOLING AND ONTARIO

Thanks to the efforts of such pioneering educators as Egerton Ryerson, Ontario led Canada in schooling during the last century. In 1891 Ontario legislators introduced a new, and for the time, very innovative law that raised the school attendance age to fourteen. Previously, every child up to the age of twelve had been required to attend school for only four months of the year. Now they were to attend for the full year and every child would, in theory, finish grade eight. The parents of truants, moreover, could be penalized.

For many children, this meant showing up at one of the classic one-room school houses that still dot the Ontario landscape (although today they are usually weekend homes or antique shops). Inside, students were perhaps crowded in two to a desk, sweltering if they were too close to the enormous stove, or freezing if they were across the room. Grades one to eight were all packed together, and a normal morning might see one grade reciting, another reading at their desks, and a third working at the blackboard.

But the central purpose of the schools was not just the three "R"s. The 1890s still held to a traditional tenet of the school system: that childish enthusiasm had to be dampened and curbed, and youthful spirit bent to conformity. As Miss Eliza Bolton of the Ottawa Model Normal School noted in an address to the Ontario Educational Association in 1892, if dogs and other domestic animals are trained from birth, should not the young offspring of human beings be so too? To that end, textbooks were designed to assist "in building up British patriotism on the basis of wider knowledge," and virtually every subject taught in the public schools had some strong patriotic or moral tone, such as the text from the period that taught spelling by using such uplifting homilies as "It is better to be good than rich."

Middle-class parents, anxious that their children be properly taught and inculcated with Christian virtues – and, of course, make the right connections for later life – were sending their children to private schools, many of which had been recently founded. These schools' character-building principles emulated the cult of "games" imported from their British models.

An 1892 advertisement for Ridley College in St Catharines, founded in 1889, takes two lines to list the school's educational aims, another two for its moral goals, and then adds five on its athletic facilities and physical surroundings. A long list of duties for masters at Ridley a century ago began with the strong suggestion that they "take an active interest in the boys' games."

(Above) Frederic Marlett Bell-Smith painted these London, Ontario, schoolgirls leaving that city's Central School in the 1880s. Most public schools were coeducational, and boys can be seen in the distance coming out of their separate exit. (Left) Members of Ridley College's canoe club in 1891. (Far left) A classroom in a Toronto public school.

143

THE POET
AND
THE PAINTER

It was a year that saw the making of one young Canadian artist and the undoing of another. On January 16, 1892, Pauline Johnson gave her first public poetry reading in Toronto. Her enthusiastic reception launched a career of readings and tours that would last almost eighteen years. On October 3, 1892, painter Paul Peel died in Paris just short of his thirty-second birthday. The contrasting fates of poet and painter, born only four months and 150 miles apart, illustrate how popular taste and public sentiment could shape an artist's career.

Born in Brantford, Ontario, in March of 1861 to a Mohawk chief and his English wife, Pauline Johnson had read most of Keats, Byron, Shakespeare and Longfellow by the time she was twelve, and as a teenager turned her hand to verse of her own. Her career took off in January 1892 when she was asked (along with other writers, including Duncan Campbell Scott and William Wilfred Campbell) to read at the Toronto Young Liberal Club's "Canadian Literature Evening." There her stirring performance of "A Cry from an Indian Wife" did much to establish her reputation as an authentic Indian voice. What would become her most famous poem, "The Song My Paddle Sings," was published in the February 27 issue of *Saturday Night* magazine.

Spring saw the beginning of Johnson's first reading tour, covering 125 towns in Ontario, and by that fall she had begun to perform in the elaborate native costume that became her trademark. Johnson's reading tours took her across the continent and around the world. In 1909 she settled in Vancouver and remained there until her death from cancer in 1913.

Just as Johnson's star was beginning to rise, London, Ontario, native Paul Peel died unexpectedly in Paris. The Canadian painter had trained at the Pennsylvania Academy of Fine Arts under Thomas Eakins, the Royal Academy School in London and the École des beaux-arts in Paris. International recognition came his way in 1890 when *After the Bath*, a sentimental depiction of two children warming themselves after bathing, took a third-class medal at the Paris Salon. Anticipating triumph on his return home, Peel arranged an exhibition and sale of his works in Toronto for October of that year. Despite the crowds his work initially drew, the prices offered for his paintings were ridiculously low and, feeling snubbed by his countrymen, Peel returned to Paris where he worked until struck down by a hemorrhage of the lungs in late September of 1892, leading to his death only days later.

Despite their very different receptions by the Victorian Dominion, the work of both of these early Canadian stars is enjoying a modern revival. Though Pauline Johnson, champion of the Canadian wilds, may have had a more immediate appeal in her own day than Paul Peel, who drew on European traditions, today both are recognized for their contribution to the development of a Canadian artistic identity.

(Right) Dressed conventionally here, Pauline Johnson adopted Indian dress for her recitations in late 1892. (Below) Paul Peel at work in his Paris studio in 1889.

(Left) After the Bath *won Peel a third-class medal at the Paris Salon of 1890, and remains his most famous painting.*

By 1892, Hart Massey (above) could boast that Massey-Harris fed the world (left), thanks to the implements turned out by his four plants (below). (Below right) The boarded-up head office of the Toronto plant is all that remains today of the once-huge complex on King Street West.

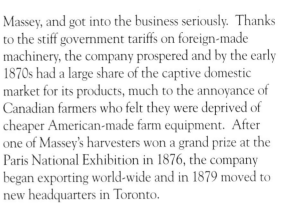

IMPLEMENT MAKERS TO THE WORLD

Today the old name is gone, changed to Varity Inc., and the company has decamped from Toronto for Buffalo, leaving behind little but a boarded-up building and bitter memories. But a century ago, Massey-Harris was a true corporate colossus, and its owner, Hart Massey, a genuine industrial baron.

In the late 1840s, Daniel Massey, a prosperous Cobourg, Ontario, farmer with an interest in agricultural implements, purchased a bankrupt foundry at Newcastle with his son, Hart Almerrin

Massey, and got into the business seriously. Thanks to the stiff government tariffs on foreign-made machinery, the company prospered and by the early 1870s had a large share of the captive domestic market for its products, much to the annoyance of Canadian farmers who felt they were deprived of cheaper American-made farm equipment. After one of Massey's harvesters won a grand prize at the Paris National Exhibition in 1876, the company began exporting world-wide and in 1879 moved to new headquarters in Toronto.

Hart Massey stunned the business world in 1891 by amalgamating his company with its main Canadian rival, A. Harris, Son and Company of Brantford in May, and then, in December, by taking over another competitor, Patterson-Wisener. As 1892 dawned, the new company claimed one thousand employees and a like number of sales agents, and Hart Massey could boast that it was the largest manufacturer of its kind in the British Empire. A commercial dynasty that would endure for nearly a century had been born.

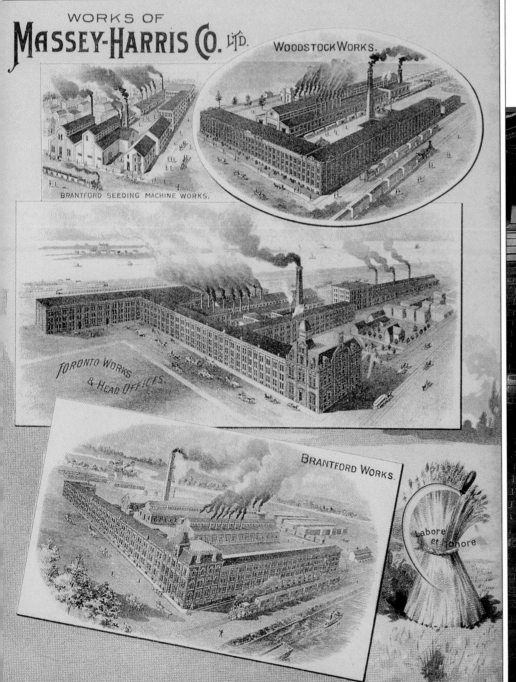

THE MARKET TOWNS GROW UP

Toronto was indisputably the most important urban centre in Ontario, but by the 1890s many other towns that had been created to serve as regional hubs for outlying farms, were growing into manufacturing centres as well.

(Right) Paul Peel captured London's Covent Garden Market in the eighties, when he was still a resident of that city. London was the big market town for most of Southwestern Ontario. (Below) Guelph's St George's Square, circa 1885. Home to the province's agricultural college, Guelph had actually been planned in advance as a farm town, with the streets radiating out from a central square.

(Bottom) Hamilton, showing Gore Park, the heart of the Victorian city. After Toronto, Hamilton was the province's most important industrial town. Earlier growth had come from making stoves, and by 1892, the city was a manufacturing centre for anything constructed out of iron – although it would be another three years before the city gained its first blast furnace and with it the ability to make steel.

148

EASTERN ONTARIO

A view of Kingston, Ontario, (below) from atop the walls of Fort Henry. Kingston had been the capital of the United Canadas at one point, and for long after that had basked in the reflected glory of its best-known citizen, Sir John A. Macdonald. By 1892 it had settled into a quiet life as an essentially "institutional" town. Canada's Royal Military College, founded in 1876, is visible in the mid-ground. The town was also home to Queen's University and to an artillery battery from Canada's small permanent military force. The round structure on the right is a Martello tower, one of a number of fortifications that had been built to repel any possible American invasion earlier in the century.

(Far left) Brockville's King Street, showing the 1892 funeral of Edwin P. Comstock. Originally Americans, the Comstocks had opened a plant in Brockville to manufacture patent medicines, such as their famous Dead Shot Worm Pellets. Brockville was also home to the company that made Dr Williams' Pink Pills for Pale People. (Left) A circus parade on Peterborough's George Street, 1889. The big news for Peterborough residents in 1892 was the creation of what would become the town's leading business, Canadian General Electric.

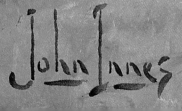

NEW SETTLEMENTS
The Prairies

John Innes

WINNIPEG
THE PLACE TO GROW

W HEN WINNIPEG WAS FIRST incorporated in 1873, breaking away from the larger Red River Colony originally founded by Lord Selkirk, its coat of arms featured a buffalo, a steam locomotive, and three sheaves of wheat. It made a beautiful municipal emblem, but its contents were both posthumous and premature. The buffalo herds had long since vanished from the city's environs, the first train wouldn't arrive for five years, and there would be no substantial grain exports for another five years after that. This attitude of glancing backwards with nostalgia yet looking forward with slightly unrealistic anticipation was typical of the place – then and now.

At incorporation, Winnipeg was not an impressive spot. Few of its streets had been planked, so that in the rainy season they were really mudslides ("a mixture of putty and bird lime"). Newcomers were warned that if they ever saw a hat floating in the mud, they should throw it a rope – there would most likely be a drowning man under it. There were so many gin mills and brothels that one journalist described Winnipeg as "one of the two most evil places in Canada" – the other being the roistering lumber town of Barrie, Ontario.

Then, between the summers of 1880 and 1883, after the Canadian Pacific Railway confirmed that it planned to run its main line through the city, Winnipeg exploded in a land boom. "The office now is like a fair," reported Charles Brydges, head of the Hudson's Bay Company's Land Department. "The people stand in a row waiting their turn to reach the counter. Bedlam let loose was a mere incident to the scene in our office. I never saw Winnipeg in such a state of frantic excitement."

By 1887 with the establishment of the Grain Exchange, to provide a marketplace for the expanding agricultural production of the prairies, Winnipeg had become the undisputed centre of Canada's grain trade. The grain trade generated so much business that seven private and eight chartered banks were soon doing a roaring turnover. Local saloons – including the Queen's Hotel, which boasted having the longest bar in the west (100 feet) – were as busy as the banks. And the bordellos were even busier.

At first confined to Annabella Street, the prostitutes spread throughout the area east of Main to streets like Rachel and McFarlane. A hundred bawdy houses flourished at one time. Their presence had the unofficial blessing of municipal politicians, though one of them sanctimoniously pointed out that the church must never be informed of the arrangement. "Clergymen are not the most intelligent of men; nor do they reason the best," he explained.

By 1892 Winnipeg's 29,182 citizens were enjoying rides on the newly-electrified streetcar service; a few years later, Winnipeg was the scene of Canada's only streetcar funeral. When Motorman Patrick Mullen and his wife were killed in a house fire, their bodies were placed in flower-covered caskets on a streetcar that led a ten-car procession from the funeral home to St James Cemetery. In

1892 the Princess Opera House (western Canada's first) burned to the ground following a performance of *Uncle Tom's Cabin*, and the first two recorded Ukrainians reached the city – the advance guard of a wave of immigration that would people the Canadian West.

In the early 1890s Winnipeg was the financial and commercial centre of the plains, exercising absolute control over its vast hinterland. Although later developments – notably the completion of the Panama Canal in 1914 – would reduce Winnipeg's importance, in those days, it was the place to be, and above all, the place to grow.

Main Street and City Hall Square.

Winnipeg in the nineties was no rude frontier settlement. The queen city of the plains could boast a social season that included balls (right), amateur theatricals (far right), and social teas such as this one (below) at Government House, home of the lieutenant governor.

THE FIRST FAMILY OF WHEAT

Canada's prairies were built on wheat. Wheat drew the people, paid the bills and even ended up on Saskatchewan's official crest. But the Prairies' transformation into the "Breadbasket of the World" was largely the work of one remarkable man and his family.

A national market for prairie wheat had opened up in the 1870s, but in 1892 a serious problem held back western farmers. They grew a wheat known as Red Fife, which gave a good yield and was excellent for milling, but ripened late. Often it was still in the fields by the first frost, which could reduce a bumper crop to a meagre harvest.

The challenge of developing an early-ripening wheat fell to William Saunders, the director of Canada's Dominion Experimental Farm. An eclectic amateur scientist, Saunders had trained as a pharmacist and then became fascinated with hybridizing plants.

Saunders started to work at Ottawa in 1888 and four years later, in 1892, sent his son Percy west to do further experiments. Percy developed a number of cross-strains, including one using Red Fife and Hard Red Calcutta, an Indian wheat. More work needed to be done, but William Saunders was distracted by other demands and the new strains languished.

Then in 1903, Charles, another of William Saunders' five sons, was appointed Dominion cerealist and began working again on the various samples. One, which Percy had planted in 1892 at Agassiz, B.C., seemed to have the milling qualities of Red Fife and to mature earlier. Marquis, as Saunders called it, overcame the problem of early frost, and even allowed wheat to be grown farther north in the prairies. Production soared, until, in 1915, Canadian farmers brought in a record 360 million bushels of wheat – all thanks to William Saunders and his sons.

(Far right) Wheat harvesting near Portage la Prairie, 1887. (Right) Charles Saunders perfected the Marquis strain that boosted Western wheat production after 1892.

REGINA
NOT A KIND YEAR

AS CAPITAL OF THE NORTH-WEST Territories, Regina was an important settlement in late nineteenth-century western Canada. Founded in 1882 where the newly-built Canadian Pacific Railway had crossed Wascana Creek and originally known as "Pile o' Bones" because of its role as a depot for the carcasses from the last great buffalo hunts, the community was home to the Prairies' main land office, the headquarters of the North-West Mounted Police and the location of the agencies charged with administering justice on Canada's western frontier.

The North-West Territories had been formed in 1870, when the young Dominion of Canada purchased (for £300,000 cash and a grant of seven million acres) all the land belonging to the Hudson's Bay Company.

Ottawa's choice of Regina as the regional capital was mightily resented by Winnipeg, where the *Manitoba Free Press* thundered: "Regina will never amount to anything more than a country village. Situated in the midst of a vast plain of inferior soil, and with about enough water in the miserable little creek known as Pile o' Bones to wash a sheep, it would scarcely make a respectable

The Mounties had played an important role in the 1885 rebellion, even (left) guarding the courthouse where Riel was tried, but by the early nineties, with the West becoming more settled, people were beginning to wonder whether the force had any future.

THE LAST, BEST WEST
Alberta

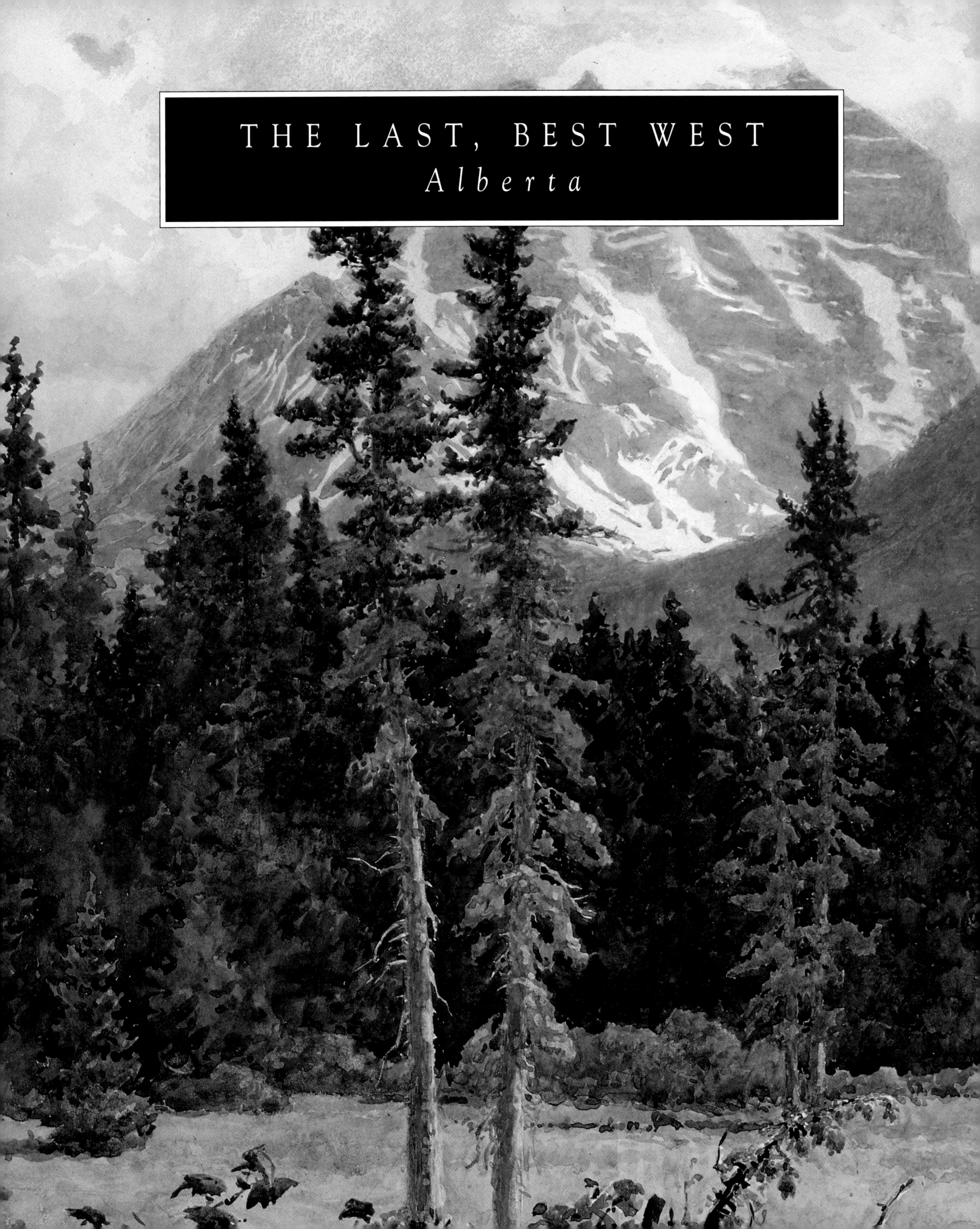

CALGARY
THE END OF THE OPEN RANGE

THE RAILWAY MADE CALGARY. Although John and David McDougall brought the first hundred head of cattle into the Bow Valley in 1872 and three years later the North-West Mounted Police established Fort Calgary at the present town site, the settlement barely grew at all in its first decade. By 1881, Calgary's population numbered a scant seventy-five souls. Then the Canadian Pacific decided to run its railway across the southern part of the prairies into Kicking Horse Pass, placing Calgary squarely on its main transcontinental line.

In 1883, once the railroad reached Calgary, the now burgeoning community was immediately incorporated into the national economy, with its population quickly passing the one-thousand mark. "Had two pieces of repairing," delightedly reported George Murdoch, a busy harness maker. "Charged like mischief, as a dollar is handled here like 25 cents at home." The area between what is now Seventh and Ninth avenues was the first to be built up. Many of the more substantial buildings were constructed from the local grey sandstone, which led to Calgary's sometimes being called the "Sandstone City." The area's most imposing structure was the Royal Hotel, which advertised itself as the finest hostelry west of Winnipeg – even if its rooms were divided by cotton blankets hung from the ceilings, instead of walls. Although the hotel was equipped with electricity in 1892, electric lights were still regarded as a mysterious force, and a notice in each room warned occupants, "Do not attempt to light the bulbs with a match. Simply turn key on wall by the door. The use of electricity for lighting is in no way harmful to health."

By 1892 Calgary was firmly established as the centre of an impressive beef industry that had spread across southern Alberta during the preceding decade. An order-in-council passed by Sir John A. Macdonald in 1881 gave Ottawa (eager to settle a region considered too dry for ordinary farming) the authority to grant up to 100,000 acres on 21-year leases, at the rate of one cent per acre per year. The first of these large spreads had been leased by Senator Matthew Henry Cochrane, whose pedigreed shorthorn herd became internationally renowned. Cochrane had, in fact, been mainly responsible for negotiating with Sir John A. Macdonald the federal grazing-land policy, and he evidently knew a good thing when he saw it. Unlike the United States, where the grasslands were open to all (the only rule was squatter sovereignty – if you got there first, it was yours) the Canadian leases excluded everyone except the lessees from the right of homesteading. By the early nineties, three million acres came under lease and one million head of cattle roamed the tightly controlled ranges. The Canadian initiative helped perpetuate the corporate frontier north of the 49th parallel, already established by the presence of the Hudson's Bay Company and the CPR, preventing the many feuds, showdowns and shootouts that were a constant feature of the American Wild West.

There was an air of Victorian gentility about Canadian cowboys. "Calgary is a western town…but it is peopled by native Canadians and Englishmen who own religion and respect law," noted a contemporary writer. "The rough and festive cowboy of Texas and Oregon has no counterpart here. There are two or three beardless lads who wear jingling spurs and walk with a slouch. But the genuine Alberta cowboy is a gentleman." (One exception was a character named Douker, a crack marksman, who could ride standing on two horses, Roman-style, at full gallop. The walls of his bachelor shack at Pine Creek were riddled with holes because every night he shot out the flame of his candle for practice.)

For all its gentility, Calgary was still a frontier town, a haven for outsiders and eccentrics who would have had trouble fitting in elsewhere. One of the least endearing local characters was Catherine Fulham – an Irish expatriate better known as "Mother Fulham" – who did the rounds of local pubs in a democrat pulled by a skinny horse, collecting swill for her brood of pigs. Unkempt, plump, and coarse in thought and language, she avoided being arrested for vagrancy mainly because police officials knew she would make more trouble in jail than on the outside. When Dr H.G. Mackid, a kindly local physician noticed that Mrs Fulham was limping, he took her into Templeton's Drug Store to examine her twisted ankle. Taking one look at her filthy foot, he exclaimed, "By George,

I'll bet a dollar there's not another leg in Calgary as dirty as this one!" Mother Fulham promptly pulled down the stocking on her other equally grubby leg and held out her palm to collect the cash.

In October 1892, the federal government announced that the mega-ranch leases would be terminated by December 31, 1896, though current holders would be given the opportunity to purchase 10,000 acres at an attractive price. The pressure to open the area to more settlers was strong, and the leasing of enormous tracts of land to a few ranchers had temporarily kept out the real farmers, or "sod-busters," as they were derisively called. By 1895, in the district around Calgary, the giant cattle companies had been replaced by farms, family ranches and homesteads. The open range of the Old West was gone – although four veterans of the early days would make sure it was not forgotten. In 1912 Pat Burns, Archibald McLean, George Lane and Alfred Ernest Cross joined together to finance the first Calgary Stampede – their perpetual tribute to a glorious Canadian West.

Calgary from across the Bow River.

By 1892, frontier Calgary was beginning to sprout the distinctive grey stone buildings that would earn it the nickname the "Sandstone City." The Clarence Block (right) was completed that year, and Stephen Avenue (now 8th Avenue) (below), could boast a number of substantial structures. Only the wooden sidewalks and open horizon maintain the atmosphere of a frontier town. (Opposite) After a disastrous fire in 1886, Calgary founded a proper fire brigade, shown here demonstrating its engine.

CASUALTIES OF PROGRESS

A century ago, it was possible to remember a time when the Indians of the West had been masters of the plains. By 1892 however, the Prairies' original inhabitants had been reduced to a life of grim subsistence on the reserves to which they had been consigned by Ottawa bureaucrats.

The official attitude towards Indians was best summed up in the 1892 edition of the *Statistical Year-Book of Canada*: "It is policy of the Government to endeavour as much as possible to persuade Indians to give up their wandering habits and stay on their reserves…. Only those brought into personal contact with the Indians can understand the ignorance, superstition and laziness that have to be overcome before the Indians can be persuaded to take genuine interest and perseverance in the simplest farming operations."

The bureaucrats' dream was that the native peoples might be converted into contented Christian farmers. Ancient Indian customs, such as the Sun Dance, were suppressed, and Indian children herded into Industrial Schools so that they could be "civilized." The discipline at these schools was harsh, and children were punished (the boys were beaten, the girls had their hair cut off) if they even dared to converse among themselves in their native tongues.

To encourage the Indians to farm, especially in the area of Alberta covered by Treaty Seven (home to the Blackfoot, Blood, Peigan, Stony and Sarcee), the Indian Affairs Department reduced the
(Continued)

(Right) A Blackfoot encampment on the Prairies. (Below) A female member of the Sarcee, another Plains Indian tribe.

(Above) The Sun Dance, a four-day sacred ritual, was suppressed by Indian Affairs. Normally performed in secret, the ceremony was photographed by Hanson Boorne in 1886. (Left) A young Blackfoot and his horse.

rations the government gave them. But the winter of 1892 was particularly harsh, and the summer harvest an especially poor one. The following years brought no improvement, and many Indians were forced from reserves, reduced to either begging for food, or shooting cattle, which caused considerable ill will among the white settlers.

After 1892 the government replaced the older Indian agents, who, whatever their shortcomings, had frequently showed some feeling for the Indian way of life, with narrow-minded bureaucrats who regarded their charges as little better than devious children. One even took the Mounted Police to task for listening to the "groundless complaints of unreliable Indians," after a group of distinguished Blood chiefs had told the Mounties that their people were shooting cattle because they couldn't survive on their government rations.

Although the Plains Indians were not destroyed, the ordeals they faced in the 1890s dealt their culture a deep shock, from which it is only now recovering.

RANCHERS OF THE QUEEN

I n the glory days of the Canadian West, Alberta played home to a true cowboy culture of unfenced rangeland and ranch hands who virtually lived in the saddle. But this new range was a mild, not a wild, west.

The working life on an Alberta ranch (or "ranche" to use the spelling of the time) resembled that of its southern neighbours. Roundups, when the vast herds left to feed on the open range were gathered together, took place twice a year. In the spring roundup, the cattle were gathered up so that the weak ones could be culled and the calves branded. In the fall, the ranchers selected the cattle to be sent to market. The roundups were brutally hard work, lasting up to six weeks, with boss and ranch hand in the saddle from sunrise to sunset.

What really distinguished Canadian ranchmen from their American counterparts were the lives they led when not on the range. The *Macleod Gazette* of November 17, 1892, gives an insight: "Last Thursday was Thanksgiving day and the Macleod Hunt Club took advantage of the opportunity to turn out in strength."

Most of the first ranchers in the area, and often the companies that owned the ranches, were English. The men who actually worked on the ranches, however, were mostly Americans, and they brought north such American cowboy traditions as the rodeo. But it was the English expatriate ranchers who set the social tone, creating a world that owed more to Jane Austen than Zane Grey. Canada's gentlemen ranchers rode to hounds (though for "cayotes," not foxes), shot grouse and, as much as possible, carried on in a manner reminiscent of their former lives in England. In fact, southern Alberta hosted the first polo match ever played in North America – at the tiny ranching community of Pincher Creek in 1886.

The genteel tone set by Alberta's gentleman ranchers outlasted the closing of the open range, thriving at least until the beginning of the First World War, and, in the process, creating a particularly Canadian cattle culture.

Roundup near the Circle Ranch, Lethbridge, Alberta, 1890. The chuck-wagons shown here provided hearty meals during the roundup.

175

(Right) Cowboys branding cattle
on a ranch near Calgary.
(Far right) Bachelor's Hall
was home to the ranch's
unmarried hands.
(Below) Many of the first ranch
houses were genuine log cabins,
like this one near Calgary.

JOHN WARE'S WEDDING

O f the many American cowboys who came north in the 1880s and 1890s, John Ware was undoubtedly the most colourful. Born a slave in South Carolina, Ware headed west to Texas after the Civil War and worked on cattle drives all over the American West. In 1882 he moved north into Canada, and before long people were spinning yarns about him. It was said no stallion could throw him and, once, so the story had it, when a blacksmith wanted to shoe his horse, Ware simply flipped the animal on its back and held it there.

In cattle country talent paid off, and by the late eighties, Ware was a rancher in his own right. The highlight of 1892 for Ware was surely February 29, when he married his sweetheart, Mildred Lewis, the daughter of a homesteading family from Ontario, thus gaining a ranch wife with whom he could share his success.

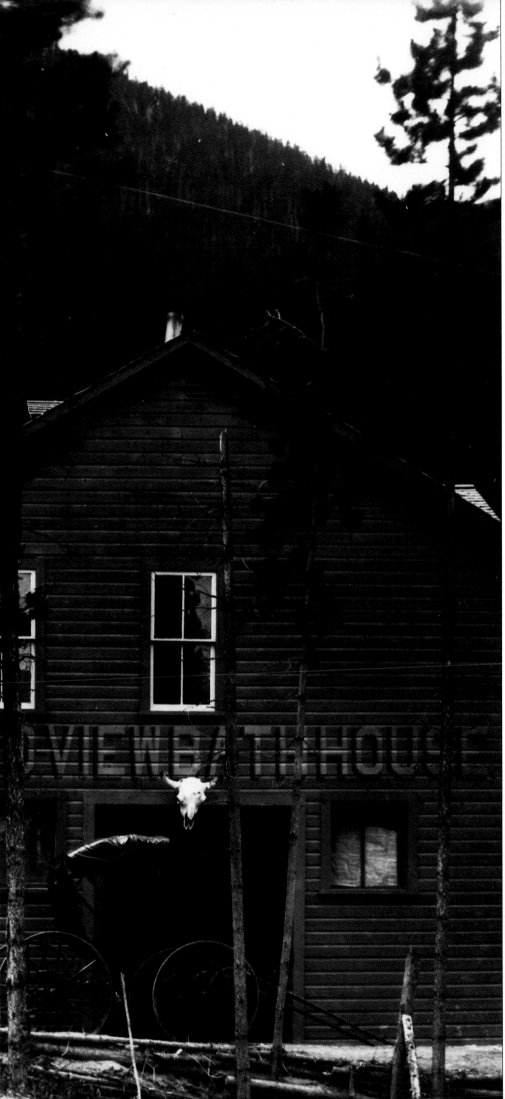

THE CANADIAN ALPS

William Van Horne believed that the Canadian Pacific Railway might be used for something other than hauling freight or transporting immigrants. He hoped to attract the kind of affluent tourists who were beginning to flock to the European Alps on vacation. With that in mind, he hired the American architect Bruce Price to build a Swiss chalet-style hotel. The result was the Banff Springs, which opened in 1888 and is still attracting customers from around the world over a century later.

(Above) Canoes on the Bow River. Van Horne chose the spot where the Bow met the Spray River in the newly created Banff National Park as the site for his hotel. (Below) The lobby of the original Banff Springs, circa 1890. Constructed of varnished red pine, its rustic grandness suited the hotel's rugged surroundings. (Left) The Banff Springs wasn't the only hostelry in town. Visitors on a budget might try the Grand View, a combination hotel and bath house.

Today, nestled among the
Rockies, the Banff Springs (left)
fulfils Van Horne's vision of a
tourist destination in the
"Canadian Alps." Over time,
further wings and additions were
put on, and in 1928 a
completely new hotel replaced
the original building. When
Van Horne first saw the Banff
Springs (below) in the summer
of 1887, he was dismayed to
note that its main verandas gave
only a view of nearby Sulphur
Mountain. The verandas shown
here, overlooking the Bow
Valley, were added afterwards.

(Right) The stage-coach making its way down Banff's main street during an evening rush hour is a reminder of (below) the Banff that was. In Canada's West very few buildings survive from a century ago, but the mountain landscape is unchanging.

THE PEOPLE'S STORE.
MacNULTY & GILMOUR

EDMONTON

A YEAR OF FIRSTS

ALTHOUGH THERE HAD BEEN A Hudson's Bay Company trading post in the area since 1795, Edmonton remained a tiny settlement for most of the nineteenth century. "We have nothing like a town," complained a dissatisfied resident in 1879. "There is the HBC Fort, then if you had a telescope and could look around the corner into the valley, you would see a hotel. Then, if there was no fog, you could see the Methodist Chapel and a parsonage, scattered houses, All Saints English Church and a few Indian tents. This is Edmonton proper."

With the 1883 arrival of the Canadian Pacific Railway in Calgary, Edmonton lost much of the significance it had previously had as a central hub in the old transcontinental transportation network that had moved goods across the vast western wilderness by York boat and Red River cart. The city wouldn't really start to prosper until 1896, when it would become the main supply post and way station for miners on their way to the Klondike gold rush. Still, by 1892 there were enough citizens – some seven hundred – to warrant Edmonton's incorporation as a town. The new townsite spread over 2,160 acres, and its first mayor was Matt McCauley, who met the town council in a room over his son-in-law's butchershop.

For the newly incorporated town, 1892 was a year of firsts. Edmonton recruited its first "volunteer" fire brigade (whose members were in fact paid thirty cents an hour). The first major group of easterners arrived (298 colonists from Parry Sound, Ontario) and in May 1892, the first immigration shed was opened to handle the increasing flow of new settlers. There was also an inkling of a future source of prosperity. Coal mines had been operating within the town limits for some time, but in the summer of 1892, the *Edmonton Bulletin* reported the existence of "a most peculiar spring north of St. Albert.... Whether or not the tar is a pure indication of a profitable petroleum field, there is no doubt of the genuineness of the find."

At the time, the best hotel in town was the Strathcona, operated by the Sharples, a combative and hard-drinking couple from Liverpool. They spent most of their time arguing, hurling invective and various objects at one another. Each evening was climaxed by Mr Sharples playing a favourite music hall epic – called "Daddy Wouldn't Buy Me a Bow-Wow" on his pub piano. With every drink he took, Sharples would add another "Wow" to his song, and by midnight, he would be lamenting the sorrows of a daddy who wouldn't buy him a " Bow-Wow-Wow-Wow-Wow-Wow-Wow-Wow...."

The frontier flavour of the town, personified by such marginal characters as the Sharples, began to change in 1890 when construction started on a

railway from Calgary. As work neared completion, however, it became clear the Calgary & Edmonton Railway Company did not intend to carry the line across the North Saskatchewan River into the main community. Instead, a terminus was to be built on its south bank. Named South Edmonton (later Strathcona) the new settlement immediately became Edmonton's bitter rival, particularly when it was suggested that the newly opened immigration shed and other government buildings be moved to the recently established railway terminal.

In May 1892, Thomas Anderson, the local Dominion Land and Crown Timber Agent, wrote to Ottawa supporting the transfer "so that the Immigrant when housed in the shed would only have to go next door to make his entry, instead of at present having to go over to the north side three miles and cross in a scow."

Having received official approval for the transfer, Anderson set the move for June 20, but when the land office was loaded aboard a large wagon for relocation across the river, angry citizens blocked Anderson's way, unhitching his horses, then removing the nuts from his wagon wheels. Not even the arrival of the local Mountie detachment (two constables and a dog) could deter the militants. Mayor McCauley held an emergency town council meeting, where it was decided to revive the Home Guard that had been formed to protect Edmonton during the Riel Rebellion.

The federal government dispatched a troop of Mounties under Major Griesbach to enforce its orders, but McCauley met the policeman just east of the town limits. "Major," said the mayor, "we are both young men and life is sweet. But if you come into Edmonton, there will be bloodshed and the first to die will likely be you and I."

As political speeches go, it was a short address but the point had been made. Edmonton kept its government offices. Eventually, as more and more immigrants flooded in, the offices became a focus for the remarkable growth of Jasper Avenue, the town's main street, and of Edmonton itself.

Edmonton's Jasper Avenue in 1890.

(Below) The first passenger train arrives in South Edmonton in August 1891. Before the completion of the new Calgary to Edmonton line, the only way to travel between the cities had been by stage-coach (right), a trip that cost twenty-five dollars and took five days.

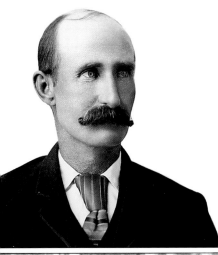

(Left) Matt McCauley had moved into Edmonton in 1881. The father of eight children, he helped found Edmonton's first school and was the unanimous choice for mayor when the town was incorporated in 1892. (Below) Donald Ross, another early settler, opened Edmonton's first coal mine, supplying the townspeople with fuel taken from his mine within the town.

THE PACIFIC HORIZON
British Columbia

VANCOUVER
A BRIGHT FUTURE

HEN BRITISH COLUMBIA RELUC-
tantly agreed to join Confederation
in 1871, it was on the condition
that a railway be built to connect
the province with the metropolitan centres of the
East. Port Moody, a tiny settlement at the head of
Burrard Inlet, was chosen as the line's Pacific
terminus, and the first scheduled transcontinental
train arrived (one minute late) on July 4, 1886, after
a 2,907-mile passage from Montreal. At long last,
Canada was truly united from coast to coast.
Twenty-three days later the barque *W.B. Flint* passed
up the inlet with 1,240,753 pounds of tea aboard –
the first of seven ships chartered to bring goods from
the Orient. Tea, spice and silk shipments now took
only forty-seven days to travel from Yokohama to
Montreal. The North American route to the
Orient – the elusive short cut that had driven men
to search for a North West Passage – had been
traversed at last, albeit across dry land and well
south of the treacherous Arctic channels that had
claimed so many lives.

But it soon became apparent that Port
Moody's geography and physical facilities weren't
equal to its glorified new stature and the Canadian
Pacific Railway decided to extend its line another
eleven miles down the inlet to Coal Harbour, where
a tiny milling village named Granville had slowly
been simmering up. This forestry settlement's
founding fathers were mostly drifters, whisky priests
and remittance men – second and third sons of the
British rich who had been exiled to the colonies.
Among them was an unlikely character named John
Deighton, who talked so much while serving
customers in his one-room hotel and drinking
emporium that he became known as "Gassy Jack,"

and the cluster of shacks in his neighbourhood was
very soon dubbed Gastown.

Vancouver (as Granville was renamed) was
incorporated in 1886, and on May 23, 1887, the first
transcontinental train pulled into the brand-new
station. The young city was very much the child of
the CPR. The railway, which had already established elaborate dock and terminal facilities, had
also built a relatively grand $100,000 hotel at the
corner of Georgia and Granville streets and had
even erected the Imperial Opera House that played
host to Sarah Bernhardt, then the toast of Paris and
London. From the harbour, the CPR's luxurious
Empress liners, their yacht-like hulls painted a
brilliant white, regularly carried express freight and
passengers across the Pacific to ports in the Orient.
"Vancouver," one local enthusiast boasted, "is one
of the buckle-holes in one of the great belts of travel
that girdle the earth."

Whatever its significance in the greater
scheme of things, Vancouver was in many ways still
a typical hard-drinking frontier settlement. The
personal priorities of the city's early inhabitants
were dramatically documented by an 1892 royal
commission on liquor traffic, which reported that
the little bush town was supporting fifty-five
ordinary drinking establishments, eight luxury
saloons and seven liquor wholesalers. The town
also boasted a sizeable concentration of opium dens.
They were entirely legal at the time and were in fact
later inspected by Governor General Lord
Aberdeen as part of his official tour.

To try to control another booming industry,
in July 1892, Vancouver City Council passed a
bylaw forbidding local prostitutes from driving in
open carriages, loitering around gates, yards or

sidewalks, sitting in open windows or smoking in public. At least twice a year the ladies of pleasure were rounded up and brought in to face the law and be fined for their nocturnal activities. Seizing the occasion, the women used the carnival atmosphere of these show trials to model their latest finery, signing up likely clients among the crowds of oglers on the way in and out of court.

Despite such rough edges (some wags might say because of them), Vancouver in 1892 was an exceedingly pleasant place to live. Granville Street, the main drag, was still no wider than a loaded wagon, but the city's 15,000 citizens enjoyed an idyllic location, a good climate, and, in the form of the recently opened Stanley Park, one of the most beautiful urban green spaces in Canada.

Economically the city was booming. A brand-new dry-goods store had been opened by Charles Woodward, and B.T. Rogers had already established his sugar refinery. The lead-zinc strikes at the North Star and Kimberley mines created significant new commercial activity, and the timber barons were beginning to move in on the virgin stands of two-hundred-foot-high Douglas firs. The forests were so bountiful that loggers perfected what they called the nine-pin method for cutting them down: they cut the smaller trees half-way through, then felled a giant on top of them, knocking down scores of trees in a single destructive crash.

By 1892 Vancouver boasted its own streetcar system, twenty miles of graded streets, three bridges spanning False Creek, five banks, a new court house on Victory Square and a busy board of trade. But progress was not universally hailed. When city hall was discussing the merits of electrification and had a sample sixteen candle-power light installed, one alderman objected. He took a tallow candle out of his pocket, lit it by striking a match on his pants and declared, "Mr. Mayor, they call this thing that they want to plant on us 16 candle power; I call it a swindle. I don't see any improvement in it over this common, single candle."

Happily for Vancouver's citizens, past and future, the protesting alderman was roundly voted down. And Vancouver could look forward to a bright future.

Vancouver from the harbour.

(Right) The angular street layout of Vancouver's Gastown, the oldest section of the city, favoured wedge-shaped buildings in the so-called "flat-iron style," such as the Holland Block, shown under construction in 1891, and (below) today.

(Left) Behind the Holland Block was the Horne Block, which is (below) still a feature of Vancouver's Gastown, although it has lost the impressive tower that once crowned this corner.

(Left) Vancouver was still very much a city on the edge of the wilderness in 1892. The dressed-up crew at left are Mayor David Oppenheimer and friends, taking an excursion on the ferry that ran from the foot of Carrall Street. This photograph was taken only a few miles from New Westminster, where William McFarlane Notman snapped these Indians in their carved canoe only five years before (above).

Scattered about the new city were reminders of the lumber industry that had first drawn people there. These bathing beauties (right) are posed on an enormous stump washed up onto Kitsilano Beach. (Far right) A real estate office set up in a tree by James Horne (shown standing at the table). He also built the Horne Block (see page 195) and was by 1892 Vancouver's biggest single land-owner. (Below) The Sunnyside Hotel in May 1887, decorated to mark Queen Victoria's birthday and the opening of the rail line to the East.

(Bottom right) The Byrnes (later the Herman) Block was built in 1886, on the spot where "Gassy" Jack Deighton, founder of Gastown, had his second saloon. One of the first red-brick buildings in Vancouver, the Byrnes Block for many years housed the Alhambra Hotel, which had the distinction of being one of the few hotels in Vancouver to charge more than a dollar a night.

As the city grew and the forests receded, Vancouver's city fathers had the foresight to retain a military reserve in the centre of the new town for what became Stanley Park. Opened in October 1889 by Lord Stanley, the park provided the town's residents with an oasis of quiet (left) in the midst of explosive growth. (Right) Lord Stanley's statue in the park today.

TO THE USE
AND ENJOYMENT
OF PEOPLE OF ALL COLOURS
CREEDS AND CUSTOMS
FOR ALL TIME
~
I NAME THEE
STANLEY PARK

LORD STANLEY
GOVERNOR GENERAL
OCTOBER 1889

VICTORIA
A VERY MODERN TOWN

ORIGINALLY ESTABLISHED AS A Hudson's Bay Company outpost and incorporated in 1862 (twenty-four years before Vancouver), by 1892 Victoria had a population of 16,000 and was about to begin construction on British Columbia's new $1 million legislative buildings. The 1871 decision to anchor the colony's capital on Vancouver Island, in spite of loud objections from the mainland, had ensured the city's future as an administrative centre – a role that successive waves of bureaucrats would perpetuate and expand. The commission for the imposing new legislature was given to a twenty-five-year-old English architect, Francis Mawson Rattenbury, who had only arrived in the city that year. It would take Rattenbury five years to complete the job. Except for the fact that the main building lacked any washrooms, the legislature turned out to be an imposing edifice.

Victoria was a very modern town by the standards of the times. Telephones had reached the city in 1878, and by 1892 the service had nearly five hundred subscribers. *The Colonist* newspaper dubbed Victoria "The Telephone City," pointing out

with pride that it had more telephone users per capita than any other place in North America. As well, electric streetcars had first sparked down Victoria streets in 1890, when only Windsor and St Catharines boasted a similar service. But the city's two lines did have a problem. The sixteen-foot vehicles, their interiors finished in ash and cherrywood with polished brass fittings, kept jumping the rails. When they were purchased no one had noticed that their wheels were set slightly narrower than the tracks on which they were intended to run.

During the last decade of the nineteenth century, Victoria's mild climate, incomparable scenery and Old World charm attracted some established British families to the city, which, in a

Victoria from the old government buildings.

sign of things to come, also became the favoured retirement home for many army officers, admirals, former Hudson's Bay Company chief factors and pensioned colonial administrators. Their presence gave the city a reputation of being more British than the British, with tea-time becoming the social highlight of the day and cricket the sport of choice. That reputation for Englishness outlasted the reality, but in 1892 it definitely meant something special to be British in Victoria.

Francis Rattenbury and a local architect, Samuel McLure, catered to the wealthy newcomers by erecting baronial mansions that were the equivalent of the British manor houses they had left behind. The grandest of them all was Craigdarroch, the whimsical castle built for coal-mining tycoon Robert Dunsmuir. Craigdarroch had thirty-five fireplaces, an imposing hand-carved staircase imported from Chicago, and a living-room that was almost sixty feet long.

As everywhere in Western Canada, there was considerable tension between whites and the Chinese community. The Chinese were allowed to take only those jobs white Canadians were unwilling to accept, and they were banned from working on municipal construction and other public works projects.

Victoria's city fathers could not believe that their rival on the mainland, the upstart settlement of Vancouver, would ever amount to much. Victoria, after all, was the Pacific coast's natural seat of culture, wealth and fashion. But by 1892 it had become clear that Victoria had lost the battle for supremacy. The city's chamber of commerce struggled to keep the sealing fleet based in Victoria's harbour, but eventually only the Boscowitz Steamship Company, whose ships catered exclusively to the cannery trade, sailed out of the port. The economic future belonged to Vancouver. But if Victoria had been relegated to the economic sidelines, her citizens could still draw pride from living in what remains Canada's most charming and physically beautiful city.

(Above) The Willows
Fairground, which opened in
1891, was home to horse-racing
and Victoria's annual exhibition.
Made possible by Victoria's
superlative streetcar system, the
Willows was built to take
advantage of the new lines
radiating out from the city.
(Below) Despite all the radical
innovations and improvements,
Victoria still had its quiet places,
where, for instance, a carriage
might draw up in a deep glade.

Robert Dunsmuir was a Scottish coal miner brought to the New World by the Hudson's Bay Company to oversee their coal mines at Nanaimo. But he soon went into business on his own and made a fortune. When the time came to create an appropriate monument to his success, he purchased the highest rise of land in Victoria and built Craigdarroch, or Craigdarroch Castle as it is also known (left). Constructed in a style that wouldn't have been out of place in Montreal's Square Mile, Craigdarroch featured the very last word in Gilded Age luxuries. Ironically, Robert Dunsmuir died in April of 1889, before his magnificent house was completed (below).

A common impression of Victoria is of untrammeled Englishness, of mock-Tudor and high teas. But one of Victoria's strongest architectural influences was the fanciful wooden structures of the American West Coast. This building style took root in Victoria (above) and persisted well into our century. One of the finest examples is Roslyn (opposite and top left), built in 1890. (Below) Pandora Street, the heart of the city's Chinatown, wouldn't have been out of place in San Francisco.

IN SEARCH OF THE GOLD MOUNTAIN

To the Chinese of a century ago North America was the "Gold Mountain," a place filled with the promise of great riches. But what they found here was usually anything but shining.

Oriental migration to Canada had really started during the 1858 Fraser River gold rush, when Chinese miners from California and China poured through Victoria on their way to the Cariboo gold-fields, establishing Canada's first Chinatown in the process. This early wave was followed by a much larger one in the 1880s, when some 15,000 Chinese workers entered Canada to work on the Canadian Pacific Railway.

The completion of the railway saw many Chinese stranded far from home, crowded into teeming Chinatowns. Faced with few employment prospects (most western municipalities specifically barred Orientals from being employed in local public works projects), they took whatever work they could get, often at wages far lower than were acceptable to whites. Chinese workers were frequently used as strike-breakers, a move that led Canada's fledgling unions to demand an end to Oriental immigration.

The labour movement was not alone in its opposition to Chinese immigration. Their admittance had been regarded as a "necessary evil" for the construction of the railway and so in 1886, after the CPR had been completed, the federal government imposed a "head" tax of ten dollars on most would-be immigrants from China. The Chinese already here were forced to send their children to segregated schools, and when employed in the fisheries along the British Columbia coast, for example, were housed in separate bunkhouses. Hostility toward the Chinese led to riots in several western towns. In early August 1892, Mounties at Calgary had to stop a white mob from sacking the houses of the town's Chinese residents and physically attacking them after a smallpox sufferer, a recent arrival, had been discovered convalescing in a local Chinese laundry.

Although they had helped to build the railway that tied the country together, it would be a long time before the Chinese would be accepted as anything other than unwanted strangers in their new land.

(Left) It was the railway that brought the Chinese to Canada. After its completion, they took whatever jobs they could find, such as working in canneries (below) or (right) as domestics.

(Below) Hanson Boorne (left) at work at Mission, British Columbia, 1892. The man on the right is C.W. Mathers, another pioneer photographer. (Bottom) William Notman (seated right) surrounded by his sons, William McFarlane, George and Charles, in 1890. Although William Notman himself died in 1891, all three of his sons followed him into the business, taking many of the pictures for which the studio is famous.

CAPTURING AN AGE

Because of the pioneering efforts of William Notman, Hanson Boorne, Ernest May and others, we have today not just a written record of the past, but a vivid photographic one as well.

William Notman's father had high hopes for his son's success in the dry goods business when he sent him from Scotland to the New World in 1856. But flour and salt held little appeal for thirty-year-old Notman and he soon set up a photographic studio on Montreal's Bleury Street to make a little extra money during the long winter. The studio was an immediate success and the quality of Notman's portraits soon made him the favourite photographer of every social class. At its height, Notman's empire consisted of fourteen studios across eastern Canada and the United States.

Landscape and scenery shots were popular in the nineteenth century, and to keep up with the demand, Notman sent his photographers, among them his eldest son William McFarlane Notman, on cross-country photographic tours to record the building of the CPR, the rise of prairie cities, the lives of the plains and west coast Indians and fishing villages in the East. These tours, which began in the seventies, continued after Notman's death in 1891, right into the present century.

Hanson Boorne and Ernest May were cousins from England, who, like Notman, turned their hobby into a profession. In 1886 they set up shop in Calgary, and like the Notman photographers, travelled most of Canada, though they are best known for their portraits of Indians and views of western frontier life through the late eighties. In his determination to record Indian ceremonies, Boorne went fearlessly (some might say foolishly) to the plains and set up his camera. Explained Boorne, "I marched in and the first part of the programme went all right." The second part didn't go so smoothly, however, when the Indians threw a blanket over the lens and fired their guns in Boorne's direction. He was later to write of the experience, "They could not see how the 'Spirit Picture' could possibly be taken of them without taking something from them. The camera must surely…shorten their lives." Boorne's persistence paid off in 1886, when he was able to take the first photographs of the sacred Sun Dance ceremony.

That any of these nineteenth-century photographers were able to transport their ungainly cameras and the heavy, fragile photographic plates of the time over rugged terrain is a testament to their determination to provide a permanent pictorial record of the vast, changing land.

211

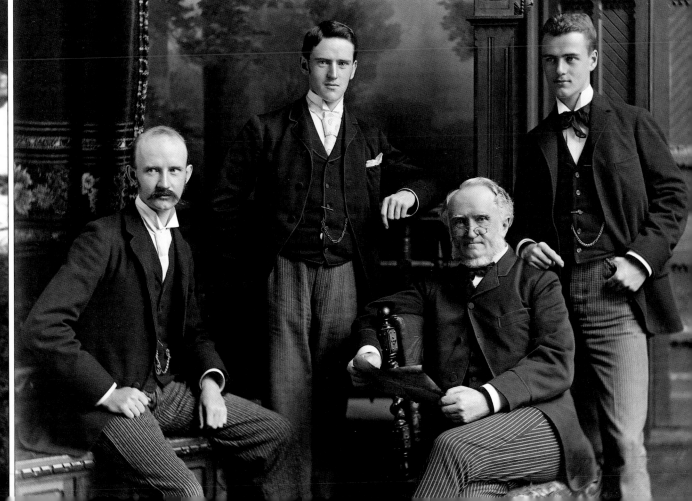

EPILOGUE
THE LEGACY OF YESTERDAY

HE PARALLELS BETWEEN 1892 and 1992 are haunting.

Facing the dawn of a new century, as we do, Canadians a hundred years ago desperately longed to believe the next century would belong to them.

In 1892 that seemed like an attainable dream. The country was like some young giant stirred by an adolescent's feelings of power, not yet daunted by the failures, misgivings and trepidations of full adulthood. Yet reality crept into the dream, too. The extremes of wealth and poverty, economic hard times, the simmering hostility between French and English, Protestants and Catholics, federal-provincial feuds – these and other trends were threatening to tear the nation apart. "We have come to the history of this young country when premature dissolution seems at hand," lamented Wilfrid Laurier, the soon-to-be prime minister, sounding very much like any 1992-vintage politician. "How long can the fabric last? Can it last at all? All these are questions which surge in the mind, and to which dismal answers only suggest themselves."

We are still what we were then: a loose federation of absurdly diverse regions that some-times feel as if they are on the very margin of the civilized world. It is an impossibly difficult country to govern – too big to contain itself internally, yet too small to yield any economic or political clout that matters.

A full century after the events described and depicted in this book, Canada remains "a promised land." There are still only seven people per square mile occupying our landscape (compared with 915 in Holland or sixty-five in the United States), and less than eight percent of our territory has been fully settled. More than three-quarters of our 26-million population is hived into a Chile-like strip lying along the northern border of the United States. Of this country's 125 cities, 102 are within two hundred miles of the American boundary.

But even if most of us no longer venture any farther north than our summer cottages, our souls are still branded by the wild. Our best historian, W.L. Morton, has pointed out that "because of our origins, Canadian life to this day is marked by a northern quality. The line which delineates frontier from the farmstead, the wilderness from the base-land, the hinterland from the metropolis, runs through every Canadian psyche."

Our unusual geography, combined with our rigorous climate, has often meant that the nation's collective moods and individual concerns are governed more by the rhythms of the changing seasons than by anything the politicians or economists might be scheming.

t is our strength that most Canadians are attached to their country not by imperious trumpet calls but by small, private epiphanies.

Yet there is among us – now, just as there was in 1892 – a quiver of common intent insisting that no matter how agonizing it may get, staying Canadian is worth the candle. Hard as we may try to devalue the Canadian experience ("The world needs Canada because if it wasn't there," comedian Dave Broadfoot once quipped, "the Chinese could sail right across and invade Denmark") our souls are branded by the maple leaf.

It is a feeling akin to the cry of allegiance of the late Will Ready, the Welsh poet who headed McMaster University's library. "Wales rings in my mind like a bell in an underwater belfry," he declared. "I am of Wales and everything I say and dream is framed in that context."

In an imported country like Canada, which went from being the colony of one empire to becoming the satellite of another – hardly daring to claim nationhood in between – it is essential to illuminate our history not as it might have been, but as it really was. Facing an uncertain future, the value of looking at the past becomes essential – but only if we learn from it.

In surprising ways Canada has hardly changed in the past hundred years. Most of the concerns animating Canadians in 1892 are still with us, and our hope must lie in the fact that however threatening these problems might have been, they did not daunt us. We are still here to argue – and implement – their solutions.

(Right) An unchanging vista. Lake Louise, seen here from the CPR hotel that bears its name, has been drawing visitors for more than a century.

ACKNOWLEDGEMENTS

No book in which I've been involved has ever been more of a joint effort. The *1892* team was headed by Hugh Brewster, Editorial Director of Madison Press, whose enlightened vision and stubborn dedication to quality endowed this volume with the magic realism that is its hallmark. The project editor, Ian R. Coutts, was unstinting in his inspired quest for the right word and right picture in the right place at the right time. Irshad Manji, who did most of the research, is a formidable talent with an unparalleled archeological instinct for hunting up elusive facts. I salute my old friend Martin Lynch, who read the manuscript with his usual eagle eye. – PCN.

Finding the pictures that grace *Canada 1892* involved galleries, archives and museums from coast to coast. Everyone contacted gave their fullest co-operation, and Madison Press thanks them. As well, the efforts of a few people stand out and deserve to be specifically mentioned:

Nora Hague and Heather McNabb of The McCord Museum of Canadian History's Notman Photographic Archives, for their help and advice, and for the astonishing efforts they went to to supply photographs when requested, even in the midst of the Notman's relocation.

Brock Silversides, and his assistant Marlena Wyman, of the Provincial Archives of Alberta, who turned up numerous excellent photographs by Boorne and May and other pioneer Western photographers found in that archive's Ernest Brown Collection.

Terresa Macintosh, of the National Archives of Canada, who unearthed numerous items for *Canada 1892*, including the colourful trade cards shown on page 20. Also at the National Archives of Canada, Kathy Gallagher-Fiebig, of the Cartographic and Architectural Archives Section, for finding the period map of Canada shown on page 44.

Susan Campbell, of the National Gallery of Canada, who made special efforts to ensure that two paintings in their collection, *A Song at Twilight* by Frederick Challener and *La Cigarette* by Edmond Dyonnet, would be photographed in time for inclusion in this book.

Maia-Mari Sutnik of the Art Gallery of Ontario deserves similar thanks for arranging for Madison to be able to use Lucius O'Brien's *Through the Rocky Mountains, a Pass on the Canadian Highway*, and for arranging for the gallery to photograph O'Brien's *In the Gulf – Deep Sea Fisherman*.

Francine Geraci, for her work in finding many of the period photographs and paintings in *Canada 1892*.

Finally, special thanks is due to Rolph Huband, of the Hudson's Bay Company, for arranging for Madison to get a photograph of F.M. Bell-Smith's *Lights of a City Street*, the image on the front cover.

Thanks also to Martin Dowding, who compiled the index and helped unearth the stories of Honoré Mercier and Pauline Johnson.

BIBLIOGRAPHY

GENERAL

Bacchi, Carol Lee. *Liberation Deferred? The Ideas of the English-Canadian Suffragists, 1877-1918.* Toronto: University of Toronto Press, 1983.

Bagnell, Kenneth. *The Little Immigrants: The Orphans Who Came to Canada.* Toronto: Macmillan of Canada, 1980.

Bain, Colin M. and R. Vida. *Multiculturalism: Canada's People.* Canadiana Scrapbook, no. 16. Scarborough: Prentice-Hall Canada, 1983.

Bliss, Michael. *A Living Profit: Studies in the Social History of Canadian Businessmen, 1883-1914.* Toronto: McClelland & Stewart, 1974.

Bosc, Marc, ed. *Broadview Book of Canadian Parliamentary Anecdotes.* Peterborough, Ont.: Broadview Press, 1988.

Brown, Graham L., and Douglas H. Fairbairn. *Pioneer Settlement in Canada.* Canadiana Scrapbook, no. 4. Scarborough: Prentice-Hall Canada, 1981.

Callwood, June. *The Naughty Nineties: 1890-1900.* Toronto: Natural Science of Canada, Ltd., 1977.

Canada. *Canada's Parliament.* Ottawa: House of Commons, 1981.

———. *Statistical Year-Book for Canada, 1892.* Ottawa: Department of Agriculture, 1893.

Canadian Encyclopedia. 2d ed. Edmonton: Hurtig Publishers, 1988. 4 vols.

Careless, J.M.S. *The Pioneers: The Picture Story of Canadian Settlement.* Toronto: McClelland & Stewart, 1968.

———, and Robert Brown Craig, eds. *The Canadians: 1867-1967.* Toronto: Macmillan of Canada, 1967.

Cavell, Edward, and Dennis Reid. *When Winter was King: The Image of Winter in 19th Century Canada.* Banff, Alta.: Altitude Publishing, 1988.

Chronicle of Canada. Montreal: Chronicle Publications, 1990.

Clift, Dominique. *The Secret Kingdom: Interpretations of the Canadian Character.* Toronto: McClelland & Stewart, 1989.

Cochrane, Jean. *The One-Room School in Canada.* Toronto: Fitzhenry & Whiteside, 1981.

Cook, Ramsay, et al, eds. *Imperial Relations in the Age of Laurier.* Canadian Historical Readings, no. 6. Toronto: University of Toronto Press, 1969.

Cross, Michael, and Gregory Kealey, eds. *Canada's Age of Industry 1849-1896.* Toronto: McClelland & Stewart, 1982.

Dicks, Stewart K. *A Nation Launched: Macdonald's Dominion, 1867-1896.* Canadiana Scrapbook, no. 5 Scarborough: Prentice-Hall Canada, 1978.

Dictionary of Canadian Biography. Vol. 12, *1891-1900.* Toronto: University of Toronto Press, 1966.

Donzel, Catherine, Alexis Gregory and Marc Walter. *Grand Hotels of North America.* Toronto: McClelland & Stewart, 1989.

Fetherling, Doug. *Broadview Book of Canadian Anecdotes.* Peterborough, Ont.: Broadview Press, 1988.

Francis, Daniel, et al. *Destinies: Canadian History Since Confederation.* Toronto: Holt, Rinehart & Winston of Canada, 1988.

———, and Sonia Riddoch. *Our Canada: A Political and Social History.* Toronto: McClelland & Stewart, 1985.

Francis, R. Douglas, and Donald B. Smith, eds. *Readings in Canadian History: Post-Confederation.* 2d ed. Toronto: Holt, Rinehart & Winston of Canada, 1986.

Frye, Northrop. *The Bush Garden: Essays in the Canadian Imagination.* Toronto: Anansi, 1971.

Hall, Roger, and Gordon Dodds. *Canada: A History in Photographs.* Edmonton: Hurtig Publishers, 1981.

Harper, J. Russell. *Painting in Canada: A History.* Toronto: University of Toronto Press, 1966.

Jeffreys, C.W. *Picture Gallery of Canadian History, 1830-1900.* Toronto: Ryerson Press, 1950.

Kalman, Harold D. *The Railway Hotels and the Development of the Chateau Style in Canada.* Victoria, B.C.: Morriss Printing Company, 1968.

Lamb, W. Kaye. *Canada's Five Centuries: From Discovery to Present Day.* Toronto: McGraw-Hill, 1971.

Macdonald, Gerard. *Once a Week is Ample: The Moderately Sensual Victorian's Guide to the Restraint of the Passions.* London: Hutchison and Co., 1981.

Mavor, James. *Book of the Victorian Era Ball.* Toronto: Rowsell and Hutchison, 1898.

McInnis, Edgar. *Canada: A Political and Social History.* 4th ed. Toronto: Holt, Rinehart & Winston, 1982.

McLeod, Jack, ed. *The Oxford Book of Canadian Political Anecdotes.* Toronto: Oxford University Press, 1988.

McNaught, Kenneth. *The Penguin History of Canada.* Markham, Ont.: Penguin Books Canada, 1988.

Newman, Lena: *The Sir John A. Macdonald Album.* Montreal: Tundra Books, 1974.

Notman, William. *Portrait of a Period: A Collection of Notman Photographs, 1856-1915.* Edited by J. Russell Harper and Stanley Triggs. Montreal: McGill University Press, 1967.

Reid, Dennis. *A Concise History of Canadian Painting.* 2d ed. Toronto: Oxford University Press, Canada, 1988.

———. *Lucius R. O'Brien: Visions of Victorian Canada.* Toronto: Art Gallery of Ontario, 1990.

———. *"Our Own Country Canada": Being an Account of the National Aspirations of the Principal Landscape Artists in Montreal and Toronto, 1860-1890.* Ottawa: National Gallery of Canada, National Museums of Canada, 1979.

Schull, Joseph. *Laurier: The First Canadian.* Toronto: Macmillan of Canada, 1965.

Smith, Goldwin. *Canada and the Canadian Question.* Toronto: Hunter, Rose, 1891. Reprint. Toronto: University of Toronto Press, 1971.

Stetler, G. and A.F.J. Artibise, eds. *The Canadian City: Essays in Canadian Urban History.* Ottawa: Carleton University Press, 1984, distributed by Oxford University Press.

Stewart, Roderick and Neil McLean. *Forming a Nation: The Story of Canada and Canadians.* Book 2. Toronto, Gage Educational Publishing, 1977.

Waite, Peter B. *Arduous Destiny: Canada 1874-1896.* Toronto: McClelland & Stewart, 1971.

Woodcock, George. *The Century that Made Us: Canada 1814-1914.* Toronto: Oxford University Press, 1989.

MARITIMES

Armour, Charles A., and Thomas Lackey. *Sailing Ships of the Maritimes: An Illustrated History of Shipping and Shipbuilding in the Maritime Provinces of Canada 1750-1925.* Toronto: McGraw-Hill Ryerson, 1975.

Barrett, William Coates. *Historic Halifax in Tales Told Under the Old Town Clock.* Toronto: Ryerson, 1948.

Crowell, Clement W. *Novascotiaman.* Halifax: Nova Scotia Museum, 1979.

Fingard, Judith. *The Dark Side of Life in Victorian Halifax.* Potter's Lake, N.S.: Pottersfield Press, 1989.

———. *Jack in Port: Sailortowns of Eastern Canada.* Toronto: University of Toronto Press, 1982.

Montgomery, Lucy Maud. *The Selected Journals of L.M. Montgomery.* Vol. 1, *1889-1910.* Edited by M. Rubio and E. Waterston. Toronto: Oxford University Press, 1985.

Neary, Peter, and Patrick O'Flaherty. *Part of the Main: An Illustrated History of Newfoundland and Labrador.* St. John's: Breakwater Books, 1983.

O'Neill, Paul. *A Seaport Legacy: The Story of St. John's, Newfoundland.* Vol. 2. Erin Mills, Ont.: Press Porcepic, 1976.

Payzant, Joan M. *Halifax: Cornerstone of Canada.* Burlington, Ont.: Windsor Publications, 1985.

Peck, Mary Biggar. *A Nova Scotia Album: Glimpses of the Way We Were.* Willowdale, Ont.: Hounslow Press, 1989.

Raddle, Thomas H. *Halifax: Warden of the North.* Toronto: McClelland & Stewart, 1948.

Rompkey, Ronald. *Grenfell of Labrador: A Biography.* Toronto: University of Toronto Press, 1991.

Saint John on the March Association. *St John on the March.* St John: Barnes-Hopkins, 1984.

Schuyler, George W. *Saint John: Scenes from a Popular History.* Halifax: Petheric Press, 1984.

Spicer, Stanley T. *Captain from Fundy: The Life and Times of George D. Spicer, Master of Square-rigged Windjammers.* Hantsport, N.S.: Lancelot Press, 1988.

———. *Masters of Sail: The Era of Square-rigged Vessels in the Maritime Provinces.* Toronto: Ryerson Press, 1968.

Wallace, F.W. *Wooden Ships and Iron Men.* London: Hodder & Stoughton, 1924.

QUEBEC

Dumont, Micheline, et al. *Quebec Women: A History*. Translated by Roger Gannon and Rosalind Gill. Toronto: Women's Press, 1987.

Noppen, Luc, and Gaston Deschenes. *Quebec's Parliament Buildings: Witness to History*. Quebec: Les publications du Québec, 1986.

Rioux, M., and Y. Martin, eds. *French-Canadian Society*. Toronto: McClelland & Stewart, 1964.

Tessier, Yves. *An Historical Guide to Quebec*. Quebec City: Société Historique de Québec, 1985.

Trofimenkoff, Susan Mann. *The Dream of Nation: A Social and Intellectual History of Quebec*. Toronto: Macmillan of Canada, 1982.

Wade, Mason. *The French Canadians: 1760-1945*. Toronto: Macmillan Company of Canada, 1955.

MONTREAL

Ames, Sir Herbert Brown. *The City Below the Hill: A Sociological Study of a Portion of the City of Montreal*. Reprint. Toronto: University of Toronto Press, 1972.

Cruise, David and Alison Griffiths. *Lords of the Line*. Markham, Ont.: Penguin Books Canada, 1989.

Mackay, Donald. *The Square Mile: Merchant Princes of Montreal*. Vancouver/Toronto: Douglas & McIntyre, 1987.

McConniff John. *Illustrated Montreal: The Metropolis of Canada. Its beautiful scenery, its grand institutions, its present greatness, its future splendor*. 5th ed. Montreal: J. McConniff, 1890.

Nader, G.A. *Cities of Canada*. Vol. 2. Toronto: Macmillan of Canada, 1975.

Remillard, Francois, and Brian Merrett. *Montreal Architecture: A Guide to its Styles and Buildings*. Montreal: Meridian Press, 1990.

Wolfe, Joshua, and Cecile Grenier. *Discover Montreal: An Architectural and Historical Guide*. Montreal: Editions Libré Expression, 1987.

OTTAWA

Campbell, Wilfred, Archibald Lampman, and Duncan Campbell Scott. *At the Mermaid Inn: Wilfred Campbell, Archibald Lampman, Duncan Campbell Scott in The Globe 1892-93*. Edited by Barrie Davies. Toronto: University of Toronto Press, 1979.

Gwyn, Sandra. *The Private Capital: Ambition and Love in the Age of Macdonald and Laurier*. Toronto: McClelland & Stewart, 1986.

Taylor, John H. *Ottawa: An Illustrated History*. Toronto: James Lorimer and Co.; [Ottawa] Canadian Museum of Civilization, 1986.

TORONTO AND ONTARIO

Armstrong, Christopher, and H.V. Nelles. *The Revenge of the Methodist Bicycle Company: Sunday Streetcars and Municipal Reform in Toronto, 1888-1897*. Toronto: Peter Martin Associates, 1977.

Armstrong, Frederick H. *The Forest City: An Illustrated History of London, Canada*. Burlington, Ont: Windsor Publications, 1986.

Arthur, Eric. *Toronto: No Mean City*. Toronto: University of Toronto Press, 1964.

Baker, Victoria. *Paul Peel: A Retrospective, 1860-1892*. London, Ont.: London Regional Art Gallery, 1986.

Careless, J.M.S. *Toronto to 1918: An Illustrated History*. Toronto: James Lorimer and Co., 1984.

Clark, C.S. *Of Toronto the Good: A Social Study. The Queen City of Canada as it is*. Montreal: Toronto Publishing Company, 1898. Reprint. Toronto: Coles, 1970.

Coulman, Donald E. *Guelph: Take a Look at Us!* Guelph, Ont.: Boston Mills Press/Cheltenham and Ampersand, 1977.

Dendy, William, and William Kilbourn. *Toronto Observed: Its Architecture, Patrons, and History*. Toronto: Oxford University Press, 1986.

Evans, A. Margaret. "The Mowat Era, 1872-1896: Stability and Progress." In *Profiles of a Province: Studies in the History of Ontario*. Toronto: Ontario Historical Society, 1967.

Filey, Michael. *Not a One-Horse Town: 125 Years of Toronto and Its Streetcars*. Willowdale, Ont.: Firefly Books, 1982.

——. *A Toronto Album: Glimpses of the City that Was*. Toronto: University of Toronto Press, 1970.

Fryer, Mary Beacock. *Brockville: An Illustrated History*. Brockville, Ont.: Besancourt Publishers, 1986.

Gillen, Mollie. *The Masseys: Founding Family*. Toronto: Ryerson Press, 1965.

Graham, W.G. *Greenbank: Country Matters in Nineteenth Century Ontario*. Peterborough, Ont.: Broadview Press, 1988.

Guillet, Edwin C. *In the Cause of Education: Centennial History of the Ontario Educational Association, 1861-1960*. Toronto: University of Toronto Press, 1960.

Gzowski, Peter, ed. *A Sense of Tradition: An Album of Ridley College Memories, 1889-1989*. St. Catharines, Ont.: A Hedge Road Press Book, Ridley College, 1988.

Hall, Roger, and Gordon Dodds. *Ontario: Two Hundred Years in Pictures*. Toronto/Oxford: Dundurn Press, 1991.

Johnson, Leo. A. *History of Guelph: 1827-1927*. Guelph, Ont.: Guelph Historical Society, 1977.

Keller, Betty. *Pauline: A Biography of Pauline Johnson*. Toronto/Vancouver: Douglas & McIntyre, 1981.

Kluckner, Michael. *Toronto: The Way it Was*. Toronto: Whitecap Books, 1988.

LaBranche, Bill. *Peterborough Scrapbook: A Pictorial History of the City of Peterborough, 1825-1975*. Peterborough, Ont.: 1975.

Metcalfe, Alan. *Canada Learns to Play: The Emergence of Organized Sport, 1807-1914*. Toronto: McClelland & Stewart, 1987.

Middleton, Jesse Edgar. *Toronto's 100 Years*. Toronto: The Centennial Committee, 1934.

Mika, Nick and Helma. *Kingston: Historic City*. Belleville, Ont.: Mika Publishing, 1987.

Oliver, Hugh, Mark Holmes, and Ian Winchester. *The House That Ryerson Built: Essays in Education to Mark Ontario's Bicentennial*. Toronto: OISE Press, 1984.

Stewart, J. Douglas, and Ian E. Wilson. *Heritage Kingston*. Kingston, Ont.: Agnes Etherington Art Gallery, 1973.

Thompson, Austin Seton. *Jarvis Street: A Story of Triumph and Tragedy*. Toronto: Personal Press, 1980.

Van Steen, Marcus. *Pauline Johnson: Her Life and Work*. Toronto: Musson, 1965.

Weaver, John C. *Hamilton: An Illustrated History*. Toronto: James Lorimer and Co.; [Ottawa] National Museums of Canada, 1982.

THE PRAIRIES

Artibise, Alan F.J. *Winnipeg: A Social History of Urban Growth 1874-1914*. Montreal: McGill-Queen's University Press, 1975.

———. *Winnipeg: An Illustrated History*. Toronto: James Lorimer and Co; [Ottawa] National Museum of Man, 1977

———, ed. *Gateway City: Documents on the City of Winnipeg 1873-1913*. Manitoba Record Society in association with the University of Manitoba Press, 1979.

Benham, Mary Lile. *Winnipeg*. Winnipeg: City of Winnipeg, 1974.

Brennan, J. William. *Regina: An Illustrated History*. Toronto: James Lorimer and Co.; [Ottawa] Canadian Museum of Civilization in collaboration with the Secretary of State, 1989.

———, ed. *Regina Before Yesterday: A Visual History 1882-1945*. Regina: Historical Committee, 75th Anniversary Board, 1978.

Charyk, John C. *Syrup Pails and Gopher Tails: Memories of the One-Room School*. Saskatoon: Western Producer Prairie Books, 1983.

———. *When the School Horse was King*. Saskatoon: Western Producer Prairie Books, 1988.

Drake, Earl G. *Regina: The Queen City*. Toronto: McClelland & Stewart, 1955.

Healy, William J. *Winnipeg's Early Days*. Winnipeg: Stovel Company, 1927.

Howard, Richard, et. al. *A New History of Canada: Movements West 1887-1908*. Montreal: Editions Format, 1972.

MacEwan, Grant. *Grant MacEwan's Illustrated History of Western Canadian Agriculture*. Saskatoon: Western Producer Prairie Books, 1980.

———. *Grant MacEwan's West: Sketches from the Past*. Saskatoon: Western Producer Prairie Books, 1990.

Pomeroy, Elsie May. *William Saunders and His Five Sons: The Story of the Marquis Wheat Family*. Toronto: The Ryerson Press, 1956.

Riddell, W.A. *Regina from Pile O'Bones to Queen City of the Plains: An Illustrated History*. Burlington, Ont.: Windsor Publications, 1981.

Smith, James K. *Wilderness of Fortune: The Story of Western Canada*. Vancouver/Toronto: Douglas & McIntyre, 1983.

Wells, Eric. *Winnipeg: Where the New West Begins. An Illustrated History*. Burlington, Ont: Windsor Publications, 1982.

Wilson, Keith. *Album of Western Settlement*. Toronto: Grolier, 1985.

ALBERTA

Barron, F. Laurie, and James B. Waldram. *1885 and After: Native Society in Transition*. Regina: University of Regina, Canadian Plains Research Centre, 1986.

Bondar, Barry. *Edmonton: The Story and the Sights*. North Vancouver, B.C.: Whitecap Books, 1986.

Bowering, George. *Caprice*. Markham, Ont.: Penguin Books Canada, 1987.

Breen, David H. *The Canadian Prairie West and the Ranching Frontier*. Toronto: University of Toronto Press, 1983.

Cashman, A.W. (Tony). *More Edmonton Stories*. Edmonton: Institute of Applied Art, 1958.

Edmonds, W. Everard. *Edmonton: Past and Present*. Edmonton: W. Everard Edmonds, 1943.

Foran, Max. *Calgary: An Illustrated History*. Toronto: James Lorimer and Co.; [Ottawa] National Museums of Canada, 1978.

———, and Heather MacEwan Foran. *Calgary: Canada's Frontier Metropolis*. Burlington, Ont.: Windsor Publications, 1982.

Fraser, W.B. *Calgary*. Toronto: Holt, Rinehart & Winston of Canada, 1967.

MacDonald, Jac. *Historic Edmonton: An Architectural and Pictorial Guide*. Edmonton: Lone Pine Publishing, 1987.

MacEwan, Grant. *Calgary Cavalcade: From Fort to Fortune*. Edmonton: Institute of Applied Art, 1958.

———. *John Ware's Cow Country*. Edmonton: Institute of Applied Art, 1960.

Macgregor, James G. *Edmonton: A History*. Edmonton: Hurtig Publishers, 1967.

———. *Edmonton Trader: The Story of John A. MacDougall*. Toronto: McClelland & Stewart, 1963.

McNeill, Leishman. *Tales of the Old Town: Calgary 1875-1950*. Calgary: Calgary Herald, 1951.

Person, Dennis, and Carin Routledge. *Edmonton: Portrait of A City*. Reidmore, 1981.

Rasporich, Anthony W., and Henry C. Classen, eds. *Frontier Calgary: Town, City and Region 1875-1914*. Calgary: University of Calgary/McClelland & Stewart West, 1975.

Shields, Bob. *Calgary*. Calgary: A Calgary Herald Publication, 1974.

Thomas, Lewis G. *Rancher's Legacy: Alberta Essays by Lewis G. Thomas*. Edited by Patrick A. Dunae. Edmonton: University of Alberta Press, Western Canada Reprint Series, 1986.

———, ed. *The Prairie West to 1905: A Canadian Sourcebook*. Toronto: Oxford University Press, 1975.

Ward, Tom. *Cowtown: An Album of Early Calgary*. Calgary: City of Calgary Electric Systems/McClelland & Stewart West, 1975.

Williams, Vicky. *Calgary: Then and Now*. Vancouver: Bodima Books, 1978.

BRITISH COLUMBIA

Abraham, Dorothy. *Romantic Vancouver Island: Victoria Yesterday and Today*. Victoria: Acme-Buckle Printing Co., 1966.

Adams, Joan, and Becky Thomas. *Floating Schools and Frozen Inkwells: The One-Room Schools of British Columbia*. Madeira Park, B.C.: Harbour Publishing Company, 1985.

Bondar, Barry. *Vancouver: The Story and the Sights*. North Vancouver, B.C.: Whitecap Books, 1986.

———. *Victoria: The Story and the Sights*. North Vancouver, B.C.: Whitecap Books, 1986.

Castle, Geoffery. *More Victoria Landmarks*. Illustrated by Barry F. King. Victoria: Sono Nis Press, 1988.

Chan, Anthony B. *The Gold Mountain: The Chinese in the New World*. Vancouver: New Star Books, 1983.

Czolowski, Ted, and Balynn Richards. *Vancouver Calling*. Vancouver, 1972.

Keller, Betty. *On the Shady Side: Vancouver 1886-1914*. Ganges, B.C.: Horsdal and Schubert, 1986.

Kloppenburg, Anne, Alice Newinski, Eve Johnson and Robert Gruetter. *Vancouver's First Century: A City Album, 1860-1970*. Vancouver: J.J. Douglas, 1977.

Kluckner, Michael. *Vancouver: The Way it Was*. North Vancouver, B.C.: Whitecap Books, 1984.

Mattison, David. *Eyes of a City: Early Vancouver Photographers, 1868-1900*. Occasional Paper, no. 3. Vancouver: Vancouver City Archives, 1986.

Morgan, Roland, and Emily Disher. *Victoria: Then and Now*. Bodima Publications, 1977.

Morley, Alan. *Vancouver: From Milltown to Metropolis*. Vancouver: Mitchell Press, 1961.

Nicol, Eric. *Vancouver*. Toronto: Doubleday Canada, 1970.

O'Kiely, Elizabeth. *Gastown Revisited*. Vancouver: Community Arts Council of Vancouver, 1970.

On Forward Thinking. Victoria: Victoria Chamber of Commerce, 1967.

Reksten, Terry. *"More English than the English": A Very Social History of Victoria*. Victoria: Orca Book Publishers, 1986.

Robertson, Irene Elaine. "The Business Community and the Development of Victoria, 1858-1900." Unpublished MA thesis, University of Victoria, 1976.

Roy, Patricia E. *Vancouver: An Illustrated History*. Toronto: James Lorimer and Co.; [Ottawa] National Museum of Man, 1980.

Stanley, Tim. "White Supremacy, Imperialism and School Textbooks in British Columbia, 1885-1925." (Second draft of recently published paper) University of British Columbia, 1989.

ILLUSTRATION CREDITS

All colour photographs, unless otherwise noted, by Peter Christopher ©1992.

Front cover: Frederic Marlett Bell-Smith (Canadian, 1846-1923), *Lights of a City Street*, 1894. Oil on canvas. Hudson's Bay Co.

Back cover: (Top) National Archives of Canada (C-24322).

Endpapers: McCord Museum of Canadian History, Notman Photographic Archives.

2-3 Frederic Marlett Bell-Smith (Canadian, 1846-1923). *The Beach* (detail) 1888. Watercolour on paper, 34 x 52.1 cm. Art Gallery of Ontario. Gift of Mrs F.F. Tisdall, 1953.

8-9 Photograph Collection, Provincial Archives of Nova Scotia.

13 National Archives of Canada (C-2829).

15 National Archives of Canada (C-6536).

16 National Archives of Canada (C-37957).

18 (Left) Archives of Ontario (S 18119). (Right) McCord Museum of Canadian History, Notman Photographic Archives.

20 (Top) National Archives of Canada (C-99311). (Bottom left) National Archives of Canada (C-136882). (Bottom middle) National Archives of Canada (C-136883). (Bottom right) Metroplitan Toronto Reference Library (MTL 892 F1).

23 McCord Museum of Canadian History, Notman Photographic Archives. (Inset) National Archives of Canada (PA-123670).

25 British Columbia Archives and Records Service (HP 36629).

26-27 National Archives of Canada (C-24322).

28-29 McCord Museum of Canadian History, Notman Photographic Archives.

30 William Raphael (Canadian, 1833-1914). *With the Current*, 1892. Oil on canvas, 40.6 x 63.8 cm. Montreal Museum of Fine Arts, Horsley and Annie Townsend Bequest, 1963.

31 George Agnew Reid (Canadian, 1860-1947). *Mortgaging the Homestead*, 1890. Oil on canvas, 130.1 x 213.3 cm. National Gallery of Canada.

32-33 McCord Museum of Canadian History, Notman Photographic Archives.

34 National Archives of Canada (PA-24083).

37 (Left) National Archives of Canada (C-698). (Right) National Archives of Canada (PA-33933).

38-39 Saskatchewan Archives Board (R-B 1416).

42 National Archives of Canada (PA-13522).

44 National Archives of Canada (NMC-105064).

45 (Top) National Archives of Canada (C-85125). (Bottom) Canadian Pacific Archives (A-8484).

46 National Archives of Canada (PA-23361).

47 (Top) National Archives of Canada (PA-160539). (Bottom) Archives of Ontario (S 4776).

48-49 F. Villers. *Tour of Governor General of Canada over CPR – Rockies*, 1890. Coloured lithograph. Royal Ontario Museum (975.48.10).

50 McCord Museum of Canadian History, Notman Photographic Archives.

50-51 McCord Museum of Canadian History, Notman Photographic Archives.

51 Provincial Archives of Alberta, Ernest Brown Collection (B.7066).

52 (Left) Canadian Pacific Archives (A-6405). (Top right) Metropolitan Toronto Reference Library (MTL 892 E). (Bottom right) Canadian Pacific Archives (A-6408).

53 Lucius O'Brien (Canadian, 1832-1899). *Through the Rocky Mountains, a Pass on the Canadian Highway* (detail) 1887. Watercolour on Paper, 101.6 x 69.8 cm. Private Collection.

ATLANTIC REGION

54-55 Lucius O'Brien (Canadian, 1832-1899). *In the Gulf – Deep Sea Fisherman* (detail) 1886. Watercolour on paper, 27.9 x 39.1 cm. Art Gallery of Ontario, bequest of Mrs. Florence L. Cody, Toronto, 1951.

57 Photograph Collection, Provincial Archives of Nova Scotia.

58-59 McCord Museum of Canadian History, Notman Photographic Archives.

61 Photograph Collection, Provincial Archives of Nova Scotia.

62 Photograph Collection, Provincial Archives of Nova Scotia.

62-63 Photograph Collection, Provincial Archives of Nova Scotia.

63 Photograph Collection, Provincial Archives of Nova Scotia.

64-65 Photograph Collection, Provincial Archives of Nova Scotia.

66-67 W.H. Yorke (English, active 1860-1905) *Ship* Ruby. Oil on canvas, 60 x 90 cm. Yarmouth County Museum.

67 Maritime Museum of the Atlantic, Halifax, Nova Scotia, Harold Lister Collection.

68 Maritime Museum of the Atlantic, Halifax, Nova Scotia.

68-69 Maritime Museum of the Atlantic, Halifax, Nova Scotia. Original Photographer: Edwin Levick, New York.

70 McCord Museum of Canadian History, Notman Photographic Archives.

70-71 Yarmouth County Museum.

71 (Top left) Yarmouth County Museum. (Top right, Bottom) Prince Edward Island Public Archives and Record Office.

72-73 Provincial Archives of Newfoundland and Labrador (NA 1578).

73 Provincial Archives of Newfoundland and Labrador (IGA 414).

QUEBEC

74-75 Paul Peel (Canadian, 1860-1892). *Marine View, St Lawrence River* (detail) 1890. Oil on canvas, 24.1 x 34.3 cm. London Regional Art Gallery.

76-77 McCord Museum of Canadian History, Notman Photographic Archives.

78 Canadian War Museum.

80-81 Canadian Pacific Archives (A-4987).

82 McCord Museum of Canadian History, Notman Photographic Archives.

84 (Left) Archives national du Québec a Québec. (Right) *Berthier-en-haut*, 1886, National Archives of Canada (C-133735).

84-85 McCord Museum of Canadian History, Notman Photographic Archives.

85 McCord Museum of Canadian History, Notman Photographic Archives.

86 (Inset) Archives national du Québec a Québec.

86-87 Archives of Ontario (L-15).

87 National Archives of Canada (C-18754).

MONTREAL

88-89 Edmond Dyonnet (Canadian, 1859-1954). *La Cigarette* (detail) 1894. Oil on canvas, mounted on masonite, 116.7 x 147.2 cm. National Gallery of Canada, gift of Gabrielle Lorin, Montreal, 1965.

90-91 McCord Museum of Canadian History, Notman Photographic Archives.

92-93 McCord Museum of Canadian History, Notman Photographic Archives.

94-95 McCord Museum of Canadian History, Notman Photographic Archives.

96 McCord Museum of Canadian History, Notman Photographic Archives.

97 Robert Harris (Canadian, 1849-1919). *View Across the Park*, 1892. Oil on board, 381 x 304 mm. Confederation Centre Art Gallery and Museum, Charlottetown.

98 (Top, Bottom) McCord Museum of Canadian History, Notman Photographic Archives.

98-99 McCord Museum of Canadian History, Notman Photographic Archives.

100 McCord Museum of Canadian History, Notman Photographic Archives.

101 McCord Museum of Canadian History, Notman Photographic Archives.

102 (Top, Middle, Left) McCord Museum of Canadian History, Notman Photographic Archives.

104 National Archives of Canada (C-7105).

104-105 Canadian Pacific Archives (A-2729).

106-107 Anonymous. *Inauguration of the Ice Palace, Montreal Winter Carnival*, 1884. Chromolithograph. Royal Ontario Museum (982.233).

107 (Top, Bottom) McCord Museum of Canadian History, Notman Photographic Archives.

108 (Top) Hockey Hall of Fame. (Bottom) National Archives of Canada (PA-68320).

109 (Left) National Archives of Canada (C-3127). (Middle)

As the capital of the North-West Territories, Regina was also the headquarters of the North-West Mounted Police, shown here at drill (right). The force also boasted a mounted band (below).

farm, to say nothing of being fixed upon as the site for the capital of a great province. The place has not a single natural advantage to recommend it."

That was editorial licence at its worst, but 1892 was not a kind year for Regina's 1,700 or so citizens. The possibility of a rail link with Minneapolis, something on which people had pinned a great deal of hope, was abandoned. That summer the town's undrained cesspools caused a typhoid epidemic. Finally, a drought (the first of a number the region experienced in the nineties) hit the district's wheat farmers hard, and they harvested only half of what they had brought in the year before.

About the only good news in Regina that year was the establishment of the town's own police force. In July 1892, James Williams was appointed Regina's first constable, the town's police work having been previously handled by the local North-West Mounted Police detachment.

The new constable may have been the busiest man in the West. The town council had specified that Williams was to be responsible for looking after "the licences of transient traders, billiard table permits, dogs and dog tags, clearing obstructions on streets, policing 'refreshment houses,' taking action on matters of public health, generally maintaining law and order – and ringing the town bell four times a day." For performing these specific tasks (plus "any other duty belonging to the office of constable") Williams was paid a lordly $50 a month and provided with one free uniform. A willing soul who was probably kept too busy to complain, Williams' only recorded beef was that "it's a trifle uncomfortable when my suit gets wet."

Regina finally blossomed into the prosperous political, commercial and financial centre of Saskatchewan, but its fortunes – and population – didn't improve until after the turn of the century.

Looking north across Regina, 1887.

National Archives of Canada (PA-60605). (Right) National Archives of Canada (C-79288).

O T T A W A

110-111 Albert Bierstadt, (American, 1830-1902). *View of the Parliament Buildings from the Grounds of Rideau Hall* (detail) c. 1883. Oil on cardboard, 23.3 x 31.9 cm. National Gallery of Canada.

113 National Archives of Canada (PA-8440).

115 McCord Museum of Canadian History, Notman Photographic Archives.

116-117 National Archives of Canada (C-5350).

118 Mrs Percy Sherwood Scrapbook. Literary Manuscripts Collection. National Library of Canada.

118-119 National Archives of Canada (PA-27145).

119 (Top left) National Archives of Canada (PA-33954). (Top right) Ottawa City Archives. (Bottom left) National Archives of Canada (PA-25658). (Bottom right) National Archives of Canada (C-1007).

120-121 McCord Museum of Canadian History, Notman Photographic Archives.

121 National Archives of Canada (C-68854).

122-123 National Archives of Canada (C-6332).

T O R O N T O   A N D
O N T A R I O

124-125 George Agnew Reid (Canadian, 1860-1947). *Toronto Harbour*, 1886. Oil, 556 x 1385 mm. Metropolitan Toronto Reference Library (T18007-09).

126-127 McCord Museum of Canadian History, Notman Photographic Archives.

128-129 City of Toronto Archives (SC 478-12).

130-131 City of Toronto Archives (SC 478-16).

134 Frederic Marlett Bell-Smith (Canadian, 1846-1923). *Lights of A City Street*, 1894. Hudson's Bay Company.

134-135 City of Toronto Archives (SC 478-19).

137 Archives of Ontario (S 2928).

138 McCord Museum of Canadian History, Notman Photographic Archives.

138-139 Frederick Challener (Canadian, 1869-1959). *A Song at Twilight*, 1893. Oil on canvas, 61.2

x 91.5 cm. National Gallery of Canada, gift of the Royal Canadian Academy, 1894.

139 Archives of Ontario (9912-1-57).

140 (Top) Metropolitan Toronto Reference Library (T 10665).

140-141 George Agnew Reid. *Family Prayer*, 1890. Oil on canvas, 101.5 x 127 cm. Victoria College, University of Toronto.

142-143 Frederic Marlett Bell-Smith (Canadian, 1846-1923). *The Return from School*, 1884. Oil on canvas. London Regional Art Gallery.

143 (Left) Toronto Board of Education. (Right) Ridley College.

144 (Right) National Archives of Canada (PA-127297). (Bottom) National Gallery of Canada. Gift of G. Blair Laing.

145 Paul Peel (Canadian, 1860-1892). *After the Bath* (detail) 1890. Oil on canvas, 147.3 x 110.5 cm. Art Gallery of Ontario. Gift of Province of Ontario, 1972.

146 Massey-Ferguson Archives, Ontario Agricultural Museum.

147 (Top, Bottom) Massey-Ferguson Archives, Ontario Agricultural Museum.

148 (Top) Archives of Ontario (S 14580). (Bottom) McCord Museum of Canadian History, Notman Photographic Archives.

148-149 Paul Peel (Canadian, 1860-1892). *The Covent Garden Market, London, Ontario*, 1883. Oil on canvas, 69.5 x 93.9 cm. London Regional Art Gallery.

150 Brockville Museum.

150-151 McCord Museum of Canadian History, Notman Photographic Archives.

151 Roy Studio, Peterborough.

T H E   P R A I R I E S

152-153 Harold Innes. *The Buckboard*, undated. Oil on canvas. Collection of Glenbow Museum, Calgary, Alberta (60.71.15).

154-155 McCord Museum of Canadian History, Notman Photographic Archives.

156 (Left) Provincial Archives of Manitoba (N 4888). (Right) Provincial Archives of Manitoba (N 7500).

156-157 Provincial Archives of Manitoba (N 5796).

158 National Archives of Canada (C-9701).

158-159 McCord Museum of Canadian History, Notman Photographic Archives.

160-161 Saskatchewan Archives

Board (R-B 1136).

162 Saskatchewan Archives Board (R-B 983).

162-163 Saskatchewan Archives Board (R-B 10794).

163 Saskatchewan Archives Board (R-B 4524).

A L B E R T A

164-165 Lucius O'Brien (Canadian, 1832-1899). *View of the Rockies* (detail) 1887. Watercolour over graphite on paper, 541 x 759 mm. National Archives of Canada (C-97677).

166-167 McCord Museum of Canadian History, Notman Photographic Archives.

168 (Top) Provincial Archives of Alberta, Ernest Brown Collection (B.3150). (Bottom) Provincial Archives of Alberta, Ernest Brown Collection (B.3154).

169 Provincial Archives of Alberta, Ernest Brown Collection (B.3127).

170 Provincial Archives of Alberta, Ernest Brown Collection (B.51).

170-171 McCord Museum of Canadian History, Notman Photographic Archives.

172-173 McCord Museum of Canadian History, Notman Photographic Archives.

173 Provincial Archives of Alberta, Ernest Brown Collection (B.998).

174-175 Glenbow Archives, Calgary, Alberta. Photo: Steele and Co.

176 (Top left) Provincial Archives of Alberta, Ernest Brown Collection (B.176). (Top right) Glenbow Archives, Calgary, Alberta.

176-177 Provincial Archives of Alberta, Ernest Brown Collection (B.88).

177 Glenbow Archives, Calgary, Alberta.

178-179 Provincial Archives of Alberta, Ernest Brown Collection, (B.9677).

179 (Top) McCord Museum of Canadian History, Notman Photographic Archives. (Bottom) CP Archives (A-1956).

181 (Inset) Provincial Archives of Alberta, Ernest Brown Collection (B.9599).

182-183 Provincial Archives of Alberta, Ernest Brown Collection (B.2396).

184-185 Provincial Archives of Alberta, Ernest Brown Collection (B.4755).

186 (Top) City of Edmonton (EA-10-1269). (Bottom) City of Edmonton (EA-10-2760).

187 (Top) Provincial Archives of Alberta, Ernest Brown Collection (B.6825). (Bottom) City of Edmonton (EA-10-1180).

B R I T I S H   C O L U M B I A

188-189 Lucius O'Brien (Canadian, 1832-1899). *A British Columbian Forest* (detail) 1888. Watercolour over graphite on paper, 54.1 x 76.4 cm. National Gallery of Canada, purchased 1889.

191 McCord Museum of Canadian History, Notman Photographic Archives.

192-193 Vancouver Library (19846).

194-195 McCord Museum of Canadian History, Notman Photographic Archives.

195 McCord Museum of Canadian History, Notman Photographic Archives.

196 (Top) City of Vancouver. (Bottom) Vancouver Library (19861).

197 (Top) McCord Museum of Canadian History, Notman Photographic Archives.

198 (Bottom) McCord Museum of Canadian History, Notman Photographic Archives.

200-201 McCord Museum of Canadian History, Notman Photographic Archives.

202 British Columbia Archives and Records Service (HP 22446).

202-203 McCord Museum of Canadian History, Notman Photographic Archives.

205 British Columbia Archives and Records Service (HP 5445).

206-207 British Columbia Archives and Records Service (HP 54796).

207 (Top) British Columbia Archives and Records Service (HP 57018). (Bottom) British Columbia Archives and Records Service (HP 30170).

208-209 McCord Museum of Canadian History, Notman Photographic Archives.

209 (Top) British Columbia Archives and Records Service (HP 31705). (Bottom) McCord Museum of Canadian History, Notman Photographic Archives.

210-211 (Left) Provincial Archives of Alberta, Ernest Brown Collection (B.993).

211 McCord Museum of Canadian History, Notman Photographic Archives.

216 National Archives of Canada (PA-16009).

223 Photograph Collection, Provincial Archives of Nova Scotia.

INDEX

222

Norman Studio

Design and Art Direction : Ralph Tibbles Design Inc.
Editorial Director : Hugh M. Brewster
Project Editor : Ian R. Coutts
Researcher : Irshad Manji
Editorial Assistance : Catherine Fraccaro
　　　　　　　　　　　Mireille Majoor
　　　　　　　　　　　Shelley Tanaka
Production Director : Susan Barrable
Production Assistant : Sandra L. Hall
Typography : Crocker Bryant Inc.
Colour Separation : Colour Technologies
Printing and Binding : Friesen Printers

CANADA 1892: PORTRAIT OF A PROMISED LAND
*was produced by Madison Press Books
under the direction of Albert E. Cummings*